Mapping the Maze

A Guide to Welfare for Elderly Immigrants

Harikrishna Majmundar

ISBN 0-9745683-0-9

Artwork by Mukund Talwalkar 1-408-224-4700

Cover and book design by Jackie Pascoe

Manufactured in the United States of America

First Edition/First Printing

"I am the daughter of an immigrant. As a former State Assemblywoman, and now candidate for California State Senate (SD 13), I work to ensure that all people have the opportunity to live full lives, to be treated with respect, and receive the services they need. Harikrishna has distilled years of wisdom into this invaluable aid for older immigrants in need of services."

—**Elaine Alquist**, former California State Assemblywoman

"Mr. Harikrishna Majmundar deserves full credit for this very difficult and meticulous attempt to provide a rational and honest approach in tackling welfare problems for elderly immigrants in the USA. It is difficult to disagree with his wisdom and impossible to question it. This book will also serve as a very useful guide for elderly people who intend to migrate to the USA, as it clears a lot of misinformation prevailing in other countries."

—**Kshitish Divatia**, former chairman of Ambalal Sarabhai Enterprises, Vadodara, India

"I have known Harikrishna for over 10 years. He possesses a sound legal background and has helped numerous welfare claimants to obtain welfare benefits. He has eased their lives without taking any compensation. On few occasions, he has sought my guidance to solve knotty legal issues of his clients. I feel that his knowledge, expertise and experience with the welfare authorities, reflected in his book, will provide necessary information, examples and guidance to all concerned. I hope that this book will be a useful resource not only to the welfare claimants, but will also prove to be a ready reference to practitioners and adjudicators."

—**Suresh Shah**, retired judge, High Court of Gujarat, India; retired President, Gujarat State Consumer Dispute Redressal Commission, India

"A valuable guide for seniors"

—**Jagdish Seth**, India Post News Service

"I have not come across a more inteligent, dedicated and true friend of the community. Harikrishna's welfare guide is a boon to the elderly and disabled seniors of Southern California."

—**Ramesh Mahajan**, Former Commissioner, Los Angeles County Commission on Aging

Dedication

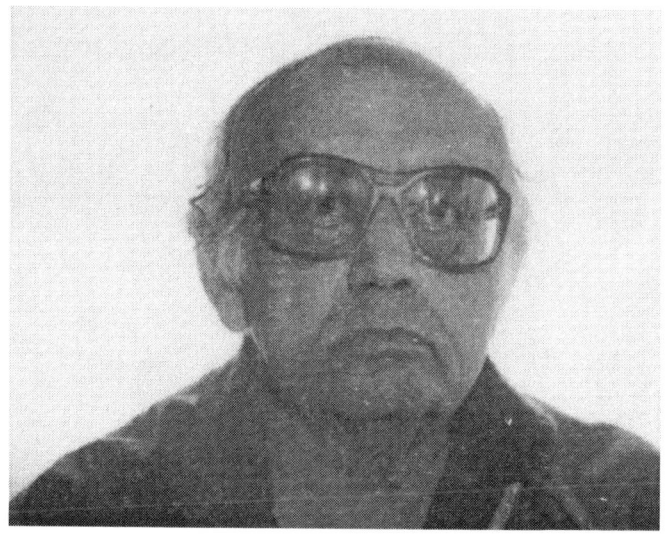

This book is dedicated to the memory of

Mr. B.V Trivedi (1911 – 1992)

A tireless worker for the rights of the poor, Balkrishna V. Trivedi helped my wife and me when we first came to the U.S. His enthusiastic efforts on behalf of others inspired me to begin my work, helping other new immigrants.

Mr. Trivedi received his B.A. from Elphinstone College, Bombay, in 1933, and then in London, he qualified as a barrister. On his return to India, he was imprisoned for his actions in support of India's freedom from Britain. For most of his working life, Mr. Trivedi was a District and Sessions judge in the state of Gujarat. He married Mrs. Shanta Trivedi, PhD, and immigrated to the U.S. in 1976, becoming an American citizen in December 1981. He died in Houston on January 4, 1992. Before passing on, Mr. Trivedi urged me to continue his work and follow his path of gentleness and courtesy to all.

Acknowledgements

At an advanced age and with indifferent health after undergoing some nine surgeries in America, I would not have ventured to take this uphill task had my niece Shilpa Majmundar not undertaken to prepare the manuscript. My wife Premlata, almost my age, my daughter Matra and my son-in-law Rajesh all have borne with my idiosyncrasies and I owe much to them for their forbearance.

Social Security Agency officers have kindly gone through the manuscripts and suggested changes where they were necessary. Mr. B.L. Rao, Immigration Services (Raoinssvcs@yahoo.com), has also helped immensely with the book and by helping those who need the information contained in it.

I have no hesitation to admit that the rough marble of my book is shaped into a beautiful statue by Jackie Pascoe. This is a case of help from the blue. I lack appropriate words to express my gratitude to her.

I cannot fail to mention my friend Mr. Ramji Patel of Uganda who is always ready to help me in many practical ways.

For his assistance with matters pertaining to Social Security, Medical and Medicare in the Los Angelese area, I thank Ramesh Mahajan, former commissioner on the Los Angeles County Commission on Aging.

Lastly I thank the Indira Foundation, set up in the memory of Mrs. Indira Manudhane, for generously providing funds to make this publication possible, and the Silicon Valley Nagar Association for facilitating the publication.

Harikrishna Majmundar

Palo Alto, November 22 2003

Table of Contents

Chapter 4 More Important Highlights 40

Chapter 5   A Summary of Social Insurance Benefits   54

Chapter 6   A Summary of Public Assistance Benefits   68

Chapter 7   SSI Rules   76

Chapter 1
Why I Wrote This Book

Knowledge is Power

In this book I attempt to help immigrants to navigate the maze of rules and regulations they encounter when they approach the U.S. welfare system.

My primary motivation for writing this book is to put information in the hands of those who need it. According to Marcia Meyers[1]:

> The first form of help that low-income individuals need is information. Learning about the benefits for which they may be eligible turns out to be a surprisingly difficult hurdle for many. Information generally available is both inaccurate and inadequate. Although low-income individuals are often portrayed as knowledgeable and savvy consumers of welfare services, research reveals that their information is often both limited and inaccurate.

Moreover, the welfare system has become more complex in recent years. Myers puts it well:

---

[1] Marcia. K. Meyers "How Welfare offices Undermine Welfare Reform," *The American Prospect* vol. 11 no.15, June 19, 2000 – July 3, 2000.

The welfare rights movement of the 1970's forced local welfare systems to operate with greater uniformity and due process protections for clients. With the welfare reforms of the 1990s, Congress revised this nascent trend toward uniformity by devolving control over welfare eligibility rules and procedures to the states. In their zeal to reduce welfare caseloads and cost, many states have used these new rules to impose more complex eligibility tests for welfare. As a result, in many parts of the country, getting welfare has become even more difficult and unpleasant than it used to be.

My work has been mostly with the Indian community, and the examples given are taken from my experience. However, all immigrants are in the same boat and, I hope, will benefit from reading this book.

The Impact of Immigrant Legislation

Some Acts of Congress have had a big impact on immigrants and have added to the complexity of understanding and applying for welfare benefits. One purpose of this book is to make these complicated rules clear. The acts, and a brief summary of their impact, are given below and explained in more detail in Chapter 3.

- **The Welfare Reform Act of 1996**, restricted access of documented immigrants to a wide range of government welfare programs (such as SSI) that they were eligible for before passage of the Act.
- **The Immigration Act of 1996**, changed the deeming period for immigrants from 3 to 5 years, and made the affidavit of support a legally binding document.
- **The Balanced Budget Act of 1997**. Some provisions of this act made it possible for certain disabled immigrants to obtain SSI

benefits (and note that most elderly people are easily certified as disabled).

In this book, you will often find different rules are explained for two groups of people demarcated by passage of the Welfare Reform Act on August 22, 1996:

* Pre-8/22/96 entrants, meaning those who arrived in the U.S. before passage of the Welfare Reform Act.
* Post-8/22/96 entrants, meaning those who arrived in the U.S. after passage of the Welfare Reform Act.

This is covered in more detail in Chapter 3.

Financial Advice

Because of a provision in the Balanced Budget Act, I can give you guidance in financial matters without criminal liability. (The provision did not cover those who charged a fee for advice, but later they were also enabled to give guidance without liability).

Thus I can provide information in this book to help you to understand the welfare rules about, for example, bringing your modest assets into line with eligibility requirements by "spending down" on necessities; exactly what is meant by contributing a "pro rata share" of household expenses if you live in someone else's home, and other provisions and limits that are hard to figure out because the rules are complex.

My Advice: Honesty—The Best Policy

A message sent through this book always runs the risk of misrepresentation. Telling the truth is ultimately the simplest way to

handle something. There may still be consequences, but they won't be about maintaining a fictitious reality or about losing self-respect because one has lied to get away with something. In the short term it may be hard to be honest and to conquer fears of confronting the truth, but it is worth overcoming this discomfort to be able to live a life of peace, integrity and honesty.

My intention is to help those in need to get the welfare benefits for which they are in fact eligible, not to help cheaters. The rules presented in this book are available in government literature and in many excellent government web sites. You may drown in the wealth of information available and not know what is pertinent to your situation. In this book, I highlight some information that I have found especially useful in my vocation as a social worker for (mostly) elderly Indian immigrants.

REMEMBER, WHILE DEALING WITH THE SOCIAL SECURITY AND WELFARE AGENCY, ALWAYS SPEAK THE TRUTH.

What's in This Book

Books on Welfare eligibility for disabled and elderly people have been written in so many forms and with such minute analysis, that one more book on the subject is a sheer exercise in futility. However, the proof of the puddings lies in the eating.

Though immigrants residing in states other than California need equal assistance, it is difficult for me to be helpful to them because welfare rules differ from state to state and at times from county to county. However the general guidance provided in this book applies to all states, and the California-specific information is identified.

During my work with the disabled and elderly I find many of them not aware of their rights and responsibilities. I hope this book provides them with pertinent information and guidance.

- **Chapter 1, Why I Wrote This Book** (this chapter), provides an overview to the book and its purpose.
- **Chapter 2, Welfare in the United States**, is more philosophical in nature than other chapters and gives you my view of the state of welfare in the U.S.
- **Chapter 3, Highlights for Immigrants**, may be the single most important chapter in the book, because it summarizes limitations on immigrants' eligibility for various welfare programs.
- **Chapter 4, More Important Highlights**, summarizes some important points that any welfare applicant or recipient must be aware of to avoid pitfalls.
- **Chapter 5, A Summary of Social Insurance Benefits,** and **Chapter 6, A Summary of Public Assistance Benefits** provide an overview of the main social insurance and welfare programs in the U.S.
- **Chapter 7, SSI Rules**, delves into SSI eligibility rules in some detail.

- **Chapter 8, Medicare and Medi-Cal Rules**, covers Medicare and Medi-Cal rules in some detail. Make sure you have medical insurance. There is no reason any elderly person should not have coverage. This chapter covers many programs, with different income and resource and immigrant status eligibility rules.

- **Chapter 9, Frequently Asked Questions**, presents a selection of commonly asked questions and answers derived from my experiences assisting immigrants in the Asian Indian community. You may find it particularly useful to browse these questions, looking for those that address concerns similar to your own.

- **Chapter 10, Reference Cases**, provides references to different kinds of legal cases, which can be cited and may be of use if you are in a similar situation.

- **Chapter 11, States Other Than California**, summarizes the welfare situation in states other than California, which is where most of my experience is based.

On-line Resources

Various government web sites are noted as on-line resources throughout the book. They are shown like this:

 Go to www.*somewebsitename*.org for some helpful information.

If You Are Not Familiar With Computers

Even if you are not familiar with using a computer and do not have access to a computer at home, you can access the wealth of information available on the Internet at most libraries. A librarian can help you to open an *Internet browser* such as Microsoft®

Internet Explorer® and type the *URL* (the string of letters and slashes beginning http:// or www.) into the *Address box* near the top of the browser window. When you click *Go*, you see the *web site* containing the information. You will find it easy to read information on-line and click on *links* (usually underlined words) that lead to more information.

Web sites also usually have a *search* feature. You enter a word or phrase into a *search box*, and the web site will show you a list of *pages* within the web site containing those terms. You'll soon get the hang of it, and will find this an invaluable resource.

Another great search tool is available at www.google.com. Type a few key words and Google will present you with a list of pages that contains them.

Government Web Sites and Other Resources

This section collects the main government web sites and pages referenced throughout this book.

California

* Department of Social Services: www.dss.cahwnet.gov/cdssweb
* Medi-Cal: www.medi-cal.ca.gov and www.dhs.cahwnet.gov/mcs/MedicalInformation/Med.htm

Federal

* Social Security: www.ssa.gov
* SSI: www.socialsecurity.gov/notices/supplemental-security-income
* Medicare: www.medicare.gov
* Medicaid: http://cms.hhs.gov/medicaid
* The Social Security Handbook (14th ed): http://www.ssa.gov/OP_Home/handbook/ssa-hbk.htm

- The POMS manual (described below):
  http://policy.ssa.gov/poms.nsf
- The text of any Federal Bill can be found here:
  http://thomas.loc.gov

WorkWORLD Help Pages

An excellent and up-to-date guide to SSI, Medicaid, and other topics can be found at:

 http://www.workworld.org/wwwebhelp.html.

This is a project of Virginia Commonwealth University in cooperation with the SSA. The help pages are provided in support of their software program, which is free and can be downloaded to a computer. The program is described on the web site as follows:

> WorkWORLD© is decision support software for personal computers designed to help people with disabilities, advocates, benefit counselors, and others explore and understand how to best use the work incentives associated with the various Federal and State disability and poverty benefit programs. It automates the computation of benefits, and takes into account the complex interaction of income, benefit programs, and work incentives.

About the Program Operations Manual Systems (POMS)

The POMS is a massive, multi-volume manual. It contains the Social Security Administration's own guidelines on how to interpret and apply the rules in various situations. The POMS helps the SSA in the adjudication and processing of all claims – and it can help you, too.

Consulting the POMS will provide guidelines and advice to help you fulfill the requirements of the many rules. Some guidelines are simple, such as keeping receipts for your expenditures, and some cover unusual situations, and help you conform to the rules.

It can be useful to cite a specific section of the POMS when helping a caseworker to understand your situation.

 The POMS is available as a multi-volume manual. The on-line version of the POMS is available at http://policy.ssa.gov/poms.nsf.

Phone Numbers

Use the following toll-free phone numbers to talk to representatives, order publications, and so on, 24 hours a day:

- Social Security Administration: **1-800-772-1213**
- Medicare: **1-800-633-4227**

Chapter 2
Welfare in the United States

Americans view the welfare state as a European concept. It does not go well with their ideals of small government, personal freedom and individual responsibility. The idea of a welfare state is seen as a violation of cherished values and an unwelcome claim upon U.S. resources.

The U.S. has been following rigid market economics. Its deregulation produces de-centralization, wages have fallen and employment is lost. Poorly paid service work has replaced middle skill employment. Foreign competitors have taken full advantage of the American policy. It is the American consumers and workers who suffer while the foreign countries get full advantage and are able to provide their people high level of social protection and public amenities.

America lags behind Europe in the size of its welfare payments, the comprehensiveness of its coverage and the spirit in which aid is given. While European administrators try to maximize coverage and minimize the stigma in giving welfare, in America an efficient welfare caseworker is one who can keep chisellers off the roll. The principle of less eligibility is the one that rules—that is, that welfare payments should be much less than what the worker would get working full time at minimum wage. This principle keeps the welfare recipient always on tenterhooks.

American attitude towards the poor has always been more of disgust than of compassion. Americans are not prepared to concede that the suffering of the poor is a problem more of structure of the society than of moral weakness Welfare reformers are motivated by functional reasons, such as the supply of cheap labor and social stability. Moral considerations supersede benevolence. Moreover, to Americans, welfare smacks of communism, which Americans hate.

Welfare rules are very complex. I believe they are deliberately made so. They are needs based. The need is quantified and kept very low. In order to be eligible for welfare, a claimant should not have resources more than $2000 if he or she is single and $3000- if he or she is married. People forfeit their month's welfare if their resources go slightly beyond the prescribed limits. Thus poor people are forbidden from saving a little each month to meet necessary expenses that may arise. Moreover for the last ten years, these limits have not been revised, in spite of annual inflation. More and more people go off the welfare roll because of irrational and unrealistic limits.

Two Branches: Social Insurance and Public Assistance

One of the main problems is that welfare is divided into two branches: Social Insurance and Public Assistance.

Social Insurance is for those who have worked

in order to be eligible for it. It is not means-tested. It is dignified and does not carry any stigma. There are no restrictions to keep resources or earnings at a low limit.

Public Assistance, on the other hand, is means- tested. It is humiliating and carries a stigma. Those who receive Public Assistance have to undergo many restrictions. They are second-class citizens and do not enjoy full democratic rights. Caseworkers have a different attitude to the public assistance applicant than they do the Social Insurance applicant.

Social Insurance Benefits

Before you apply for Public Assistance benefits, you must apply for any Social Insurance benefits you are entitled to. In the category of Social Insurance benefits are:

- Social Security
- Unemployment Insurance
- Disability Insurance
- Worker's Compensation
- Medicare
- Earned Income Credits

See Chapter 5 on page 54 for more details.

Public Assistance Benefits

Public Assistance benefits are a patchwork of different, often overlapping programs. Each may have different eligibility requirements, and programs can vary from state to state. This book provides some helpful guidelines on this topic. The main programs are:

- Supplemental Security Income (SSI)
- Medicaid, which is called Medi-Cal in California
- Food Stamps (Federal, and State)
- General Assistance
- In-home Assistance
- Rent Relief and Housing Subsidies
- Temporary Assistance for Needy Families (TANF)
- Subsidized lunch, meals-on-wheels, and many other miscellaneous benefits

See Chapter 6 on page 68 for a description of these programs, and the chapters following for more detail on how to determine if you qualify for them.

Work is Worship

Work is Worship may be a platitude elsewhere but in America it is practiced by successful people at all levels. This is praiseworthy. The American Dream is of going from rags to riches. This dream includes a belief that anyone—anyone at all, no matter how poor, unfortunate or disadvantaged—can succeed in life merely by grabbing whatever opportunity comes along and working hard at it.

It is natural for many to genuinely believe that public welfare harms those who receive it more than it helps them. How? A person's labor, and willingness and ability to work, is his or her own. If government offers poor people welfare, it deprives them of the necessity to work as hard as possible in order to support themselves and their families, that is, to sell their labor in exchange for wages. With that loss people also lose individuality and a sense of initiative; their very independence is gone. Hilaire Bellock termed the welfare state a servile state, where the poor welfare recipients are slaves in the sense that they own nothing but a license to earn a living revocable by someone else.

This may sound a little strange, because American capitalism has broken a moral code, which consists of three promises based on the individual's willingness to work:

* First any adult willing to work full time deserves a full time job.
* Second, that job should pay enough to lift that person and his or her family out of poverty.
* Third, people should have the opportunity to move beyond this bare minimum by making full use of their talents and abilities.

On these three promises rests almost every aspect of the modern social contract that still survives. Even the moral basis of welfare reforms are based on them.

The war on dependence, the devolution of public authority and the application of market models of public policy hasten the collapse of the welfare program. In a capitalist economy it is necessary that there should be a pool of unemployed workers from which labor may be hired when required. The application of market models of public policy and globalization make capital move to locations of highest profit in a trice. Labor has no such privilege. The corporation, in order to avoid liability, resorts to part-time labor in the education, entertainment, and service sectors. The privatization of welfare would mean that the market would determine benefits available, with the goal of reducing numbers on welfare rolls rather than providing assistance to needy people. It is sad to conclude that the bell tolls for the American Welfare Program.

The Historical Perspective

The eminent historian Paul Johnson in his book *A History Of the American People* raises some thought-provoking questions:

> The creation of the United States of America is the greatest of all human adventures. No other national story holds such tremendous lessons for the American People, themselves and for the rest of mankind. It now spans four centuries and as we have entered the new millennium, we need to retell it, for if we can learn these lessons and build upon them, the whole humanity will benefit in the new age which is now opening.

> American history raises three fundamental questions. First, can a nation rise above the injustices of its origin and by its moral purpose and performance atone for them? All nations are born in war, conquest and crime, usually concealed by the obscurity of the distant past. The United States, from its earliest colonial times, won its title deeds in the dispossession of an indigenous people, and the securing of self-sufficiency through the sweat and pain of an enslaved race. In the judgmental scales of history, such grievous wrongs must be balanced by the erection of a society dedicated to justice and fairness. Has the United States done this? Has it expiated its original sins?

> The second question provides the key to the first. In the process of nation building, can ideals and altruism-the desire to build the perfect community-be mixed successfully with acquisitiveness and ambition, without which no dynamic society can be built at all? Have the Americans got the mixture right? Have they forged a

nation where righteousness has an edge over the needful self-interest?

Thirdly the Americans originally aimed to build an otherworldly "City on a Hill" but found themselves designing a republic of the people, to be a model for the entire planet. Have they made good their audacious claims? Have they indeed proved exemplars for humanity? And will they continue to be so in the new millennium?

Further Reading

Gilens, Martin, *Why Americans Hate Welfare*, (Chicago UP, 1999)

Katz, Michael B., *The Price of Citizenship: Redefining The American Welfare State*, (Henry Holt, 2002)

Kronenwetter, Michael, *Welfare State America: Safety Net or Social Contract?* (Franklin Watts, 1993)

Kuttner, Robert (Ed.), *Making Work Pay America After Welfare*, (The New Press, 2002)

Johnson, Paul, *A History of the American People*, (Harper Perennial, 1999)

Annual Statistical Supplement, 2001: Social Security Bulletin, (www.ssa.gov/policy/docs/statcomps/)

McCormick, Harvey, *Social Security Claims and Procedures*, (West Publishing, 1991)

Chapter 3
Highlights for Immigrants

Because of changes in rules, especially in the late 1990s, it is important to understand how the date of your immigration, the affidavit of support signed by your sponsor, your age, and your disability status affect your eligibility for various welfare programs.

 Go to http://www.bcis.gov/graphics/formsfee/forms/i-864pkg.htm to see form I-864, the Affidavit of Support, and supplementary information.

This chapter contains sections on the following:

- The Impact of Legislation, page 18
- Public Charge Rules, page 24
- Eligibility for SSI, page 25
- Disability and Eligibility for SSI, page 28
- Eligibility for CAPI on page 33
- Age-Out Protection for Minor Immigrants, page 34
- Deeming Period Rules in California, page 36

For all programs, see Table 1 for a summary of basic eligibility requirements and Table 2 for deeming periods.

The Impact of Legislation

This section outlines two important Acts of Congress that affect immigrants, the Welfare Reform Act of 1996, and the Immigration Act of 1996.

- Go to http://www.nilc.org/ciwc/tbls_other-mats/Cal_Bs_Table.PDF for a useful summary of immigrant eligibility for various programs.

- Go to http://www.pai-ca.org/pubs/539001.pdf for another excellent summary of immigrant eligibility requirements for various programs

- This government web site is also current and summarizes the restrictions on immigrants: http://aspe.hhs.gov/hsp/immigration/restrictions-sum.htm

Pre-8/22/96 and Post-8/22/96 Entrants

In this book, you will often find different rules are explained for pre-8/22/96, and post-8/22/96 entrants, and for some transitional groups. This is because of the impact of the Welfare Reform Act and the Immigration Act, explained in greater detail below.

Traditional and New Affidavit of Support

The traditional affidavit of support was not a legally binding agreement. It stated that the sponsor would support the immigrant for 3 years, so the immigrant would not become a public charge. The new affidavit is a legally binding document. It lengthens the sponsorship period from 3 to 5 years.

Post-8/22/96 Entrants whose Sponsors Signed the Traditional Affidavit

Those who arrived in the transitional period, after 8/22/96 but before the end of 1997 are in a special case. This is because their sponsors signed the old affidavit of support. The form for the new affidavit of support was not available until December 19, 1997. The traditional agreement (affidavit of support) requires a 3-year deeming period (instead of the current 5 years) and that agreement wasn't a binding legal statement (but the current one is legally binding).

Those who are "grandfathered"

Some immigrants fall within the Welfare Reform Act's grandfather clause. For example, those who arrived before 8/22/96 and received SSI at any time prior to that date remain eligible to receive SSI if they meet requirements, even if they were not receiving SSI on 8/22/96.

The Welfare Reform Act of 1996

The full name of this important Act of Congress is the Personal Responsibility and Work Opportunity Reconciliation Act of 1996, Pub. L. No. 104-193, 110 Stat. 2105, 104th Cong., 2d Session. (Aug. 22, 1996). But (fortunately) it is better known as the Welfare Reform Act for short.

The main aim of this Act is to encourage those on welfare to return to work. However it also has provisions that specifically affect immigrants:

> The law includes provisions that would deny most forms of public assistance to most legal immigrants for five years or until they attain citizenship. The President has said that legal immigrants who fall on hard times through no fault of their own and need help should get it, although their sponsors should take additional responsibility for them.[2]

The aim of these provisions is to prevent unscrupulous people from immigrating to the U.S.A with the intention of immediately

---

2 http://www.acf.dhhs.gov/programs/opa/facts/prwora96.htm

becoming a public charge. Those who immigrate should have a modicum of independence, and their sponsoring family member should take on responsibility for their welfare for the first few years, until such time as the immigrant can become a citizen of the U.S

Unfortunately, many elderly immigrants have little chance of becoming American citizens, whether because of language difficulties, or disabilities incidental to old age.

The Welfare Reform Act has restricted access of documented immigrants to a wide range of government programs such as food stamps, supplemental security income, Medicaid, Medicare, assisted housing, and educational grants. For example, before passage of the Welfare Reform Act, Supplemental Security Income (SSI) was available to non-citizens who were legally admitted to the United States, once the sponsor deeming period was complete.

⮌ The *deeming* period is the period during which a sponsor's income and resources are deemed to be those of the sponsored immigrant for the purpose of determining eligibility for welfare.

Many other changes were introduced by this Act, adding complexity to an already complicated situation.

Various supplementary programs and amendments to the act have made it possible for non-citizens in need to receive some benefits from the government. This is also complex, and varies by state, and in this book I attempt to explain the situation in California. Often caseworkers themselves do not know all the rules that apply to elderly immigrants.

The Immigration Act of 1996

Title V of the Immigration Act changed the deeming rules for immigrants. The deeming period became 5 years instead of three, and the new affidavit of support is legally binding, whereas the old affidavit was not.

The "traditional" affidavit of support used INS form I –134. The "new" affidavit of support uses INS form I-864. The new affidavit of support went into use on December 19, 1997 as a provision of the Immigration Act.

 Go to http://www.bcis.gov/graphics/formsfee/forms/i-864pkg.htm to see form I-864, the Affidavit of Support, and supplementary information

Between 8/22/96 and December 19, 1997, the traditional affidavit of support was used because the new form was not yet ready for use. A grandfather clause covers immigrants who used the traditional affidavit during this period.

Here is an excerpt from Title V of the Illegal Immigration Reform and Immigrant Responsibility Act of 1996 Pub. L. 104- 208, 110 Stat. 3009 (IIRIRA) (called the Immigration Act for short):

> [The Act] contains amendments to the welfare bill, the Social Security Act, and INA [*Immigration and Nationality Act*] which are directed at limiting aliens' access to public benefits. Proof of citizenship is required to receive public benefits and verification of immigration status is required for Social Security and higher-educational assistance. A transition period (until April 1, 1997) is established for aliens who are currently receiving food stamps.
>
> The requirements for an affidavit of support for sponsored immigrants are tightened and that document is defined as an enforceable contract. The deeming requirements for attribution of a sponsor's income and resources are narrowed (at least 125 percent of the Federal Poverty Line). States are authorized to deem income of the sponsor for the purposes of benefits under means-tested programs, to limit assistance to aliens, and to distinguish among

classes of aliens in providing general cash public assistance. Several verification and eligibility requirements are established for receipt of housing assistance or other financial assistance related to housing.

The above quotations come from this resource:
www.immigration.gov/graphics/publicaffairs/factsheets/948.htm

Go to this web site for more details about the impact on eligibility:
www.familiesusa.org/site/DocServer/immigrants.pdf?docID=365

The Balanced Budget Act of 1997

On August 5, 1997, P.L. 105-33, the Balanced Budget Act of 1997, amended the Welfare Reform Act of 1996, and added additional alien eligibility criteria. According to the POMS manual:

The 1997 law also provided that most qualified aliens who were receiving SSI benefits on 8/22/96 would have their alien eligibility (and, as a result, their SSI benefits) continued, provided all other eligibility requirements were met. The alien eligibility of these individuals was "grandfathered."

Text taken from http://policy.ssa.gov/poms.nsf/lnx/0500502001

Go to http://thomas.loc.gov/cgi-bin/query/z?c105:H.R.2015.ENR: for more details. Include the closing colon (:).

The term "qualified alien" also known as "qualified immigrant" generally means lawful permanent residents (LPRs). See footnote 1 to Table 1 on page 37 for a full definition.

The Noncitizen Benefit Clarification (etc) Act of 1998

On 10/28/1998, P.L. 105-306, the Noncitizen Benefit Clarification and Other Technical Amendments Act of 1998 took effect. As an effect, more aliens whose SSI was discontinued as a result of the

Welfare Reform Act were again made eligible, or their continued eligibility was assured:

> On 10/28/98, P.L. 105-306, the Noncitizen Benefit Clarification and Other Technical Amendments Act of 1998, further changed the SSI alien eligibility rules by "grandfathering" nonqualified aliens who were receiving SSI benefits on 8/22/96. These were aliens who had been receiving SSI on 8/22/96 based on a determination that they were permanently residing in the U.S. under color of law (PRUCOL).

Further:

> Under the new criteria, "qualified" aliens who were lawfully residing in the United States on August 22, 1996, and who are disabled or blind as defined in section 1614(a) of the Social Security Act are eligible for benefits under title XVI (of the Social Security Act) provided all other eligibility requirements are met. Individuals can establish eligibility based on disability or blindness at any age, even on or after attaining age 65.

⮑ Many caseworkers are unfamiliar with these provisions of the law. They assume that those over retirement age are not eligible for disability benefits. In fact, this is true only of those entitled to Social Security benefits.

In addition to qualified aliens, determinations of disability under title XVI also may be needed for other individuals age 65 or older to determine: State supplements in some states (Section 1616 of the Act); Whether the work incentive provisions of section 1619(b) of the Act are applicable; or Appropriate deeming of income and resources (section 1621(f)(1) of the Act; 20 CFR 416.1160, 416.1161, 416.1166a, and 416.1204).

🕸 Go to http://thomas.loc.gov/cgi-bin/bdquery/z?d105:H.R4558: for the full text of the Act. Include the closing colon (:).

Public Charge Rules

When you immigrate, your sponsor promises that you will not become a *public charge* during the deeming period – that is, that you will not come in the country and immediately use up the country's welfare resources. A prospective immigrant who is likely to become a public charge is not admissible to the United States.

This provision particularly affects California because it is a home to one third of all immigrants. According to 2000 census report, the population of North America is a little more than 280 Millions, out of which the share of California is 34 Millions. The share of Asian Indians is 0.315 Millions. On the basis of the National Average of 12 percent, the elderly population of Indian immigrants would be about 40 thousand.

⮑ Did you know that after 15 years of residency, you are exempt from the English language requirement for citizenship?

What is "Cash Assistance?"

For the purpose of determining who is a "public charge," cash assistance for income maintenance includes CAPI, SSI, TANF, but does not include supplementary cash benefits excluded from the term "Assistance" under TANF program rules, or any non-cash benefits and services provided by the TANF program.

Receipt of Medi-Cal Benefits – Not a Public Charge

It is important for you to clearly understand that receipt of Medi-Cal is not considered a public charge. Therefore, if you cannot afford to purchase private health insurance – and this is very likely if you are an elderly person because it is hard to come by and expensive – you can and should apply for Medi-Cal coverage. You can apply as soon as you have status with the BCIS. No one should be without basic health care!

Other Programs Not Considered Public Charges

You can also receive the following benefits without being considered a public charge:

* Children Health Insurance Program (CHIP)
* Nutrition Program including Food Stamps
* Housing assistance
* Children's services and energy assistance
* Education assistance
* Job training program
* In-kind community based program

Eligibility for SSI

For the most part, only citizens are eligible for SSI. Non-citizens have been excluded by various legislative actions. Read this section to understand if you are eligible or not. If you are not eligible because of your immigration status, you may be covered by CAPI, which is explained after SSI.

Rules for non-citizens: www.ssa.gov/pubs/11051.html

http://www.socialsecurity.gov/notices/supplemental-security-income/spotlights/spot-non-citizens.htm

http://aspe.hhs.gov/hsp/immigration/restrictions-sum.htm

⊃ If you are eligible for SSI except for immigration status, you are also eligible for Medi-Cal. Those with more income are also eligible for some Medi-Cal programs. It is important to have health insurance!

Categories of Eligible Immigrants

As a non-citizen, you are eligible for SSI only if you meet all income and resource eligibility criteria and you fall in any of these categories:

* You are a pre-8/22/96 entrant, and you were over 65 before 8/22/96 (Grandfather clause).

* You are a pre-8/22/96 entrant, you were not 65 when you arrived, and you became disabled after you arrived in the U.S.

* You are a post-8/22/96 entrant, but you signed the traditional affidavit, and the 3-year deeming period is complete, and you became disabled *after* arriving in the U.S.

* You are fully insured (40 credits) and have completed 5 years residency. The amount of your insurance will be small. You are eligible for SSI to supplement your SS. See following sections for more on this topic.

⊃ See "Disability and Eligibility for SSI" on page 28 for more information on the disability criterion, which can greatly help many elderly immigrants to qualify for needed benefits.

Those Who Are Fully Insured (Have 40 Credits)

⊃ Under a recent ruling, if you are a non-citizen and are fully insured, you are eligible for SSI.

If you are fully insured, you qualify for Social Security. To be fully insured, you need 40 credits, also known as quarters. One credit is given for each quarter (three month period) worked, or for a certain amount in income, regardless of when earned. You don't have to be a citizen to be eligible for Social Security.

Counting credits for the purpose of determining SSI eligibility has a few extra rules, which are given in the next section.

If the amount of the Social Security payment is small, you can get SSI to supplement it if you are otherwise eligible.

For those who arrived (and obtained status with the BCIS) before 8/22/96, there is no exclusion period (because the three year deeming period is complete). If you arrived after 8/22/96, you are not eligible for this SSI supplement until 5 years after your entry to the U.S. as a qualified alien.

How to Count Credits for SSI Eligibility

Effect of Cash Welfare Benefits on Counting Credits for SSI

Any quarters (after 8/22/96) during which you or anyone in your immediate family received any cash welfare benefit are not counted as qualifying quarters for SSI eligibility. (They do, however, count for Social Security eligibility.) Cash welfare benefits include: SSI, Medicaid (but NOT Medi-Cal), Food Stamps, and TANF. Medi-Cal does not count because it is not a cash benefit. In some states, Medicaid is provided as a cash benefit.

Combining Credits for SSI Eligibility

As usual, the details of the rules are complex, but these are the general guidelines that cover most cases.

You can combine credits with those of your spouse to come up with the 40-credit minimum for SSI eligibility. (You can't combine credits for any other reason.) For example, if you have 19 and your spouse has 21, you are *both* considered to have 40 credits, for the purposes of assessing your SSI eligibility. You can combine credits with a deceased spouse's credits (but not a divorced spouse's credits). You can even combine your credits with a deceased spouse's credits *and* those of your current spouse if you remarried.

At any age, you can also combine your credits with credits earned by your parent (including an adoptive parent) while you were under 18. This is true even if your parent is now deceased. The rule applies to stepparents as long as the marriage has not been annulled or dissolved and your stepparent was married to your parent when the credits were earned.

You can combine credits with those of your spouse *and* your parent (as specified above) to reach the 40-credit threshold.

Disability and Eligibility for SSI

As explained in the section the section "Categories of Eligible Immigrants" on page 26, most non-citizens are not eligible for SSI. However, some exceptions are made for immigrants who signed the traditional affidavit and who became disabled after 8/22/96.

> Based on the government definition of disability, most elderly people are considered disabled. Therefore many elderly immigrants who are otherwise eligible can receive SSI, as well as Medi-Cal.

"But I'm Not Disabled!"

The SSA does not define disability in the ordinary way. The SSA defines disability simply as the inability to work continuously for 12 months.

You may think that you have to be bedridden to be considered disabled. This is not so. Do not judge for yourself whether you are disabled. Your personal pride may get in the way. You may not consider yourself to be a disabled person, but under government definitions, you may qualify for SSI benefits because of disability.

 And, perhaps even more importantly, if you qualify for SSI, you qualify for Medi-Cal.

For example, bad eyesight itself is not a disability, unless you are determined to be legally blind. Deafness by itself is not considered a disability. However, if you have *both* very bad eyesight, *and* are very hard of hearing, you may be considered as disabled for work.

To qualify as a disabled person, you need medical certification. When you apply for disability benefits, you will receive a medical examination **at no charge to yourself** to determine your disability.——

You can also claim disability if you cannot speak English, because illiteracy (in English) is considered a disability, especially in combination with another disability.

If you have certain ailments – the SSA maintains a list of these ailments – you are *automatically* considered disabled. For example, extremely obese people are considered disabled.

So it's worth your time to find out if you are in fact disabled, in the government's sense of the word.

The SSA Definition of Disability

Here are some excerpts from the Social Security Act so you can read in the government's own words how they define disability:

> Inability to engage in any substantial gainful activity by reason of any medically determinable physical or mental impairment which can be expected to result in death or which has lasted or can be expected to last for a continuous period of not less than 12 months.

 The text can be read here:
http://www.ssa.gov/OP_Home/ssact/title16b/1600.htm

How Disability is Evaluated in the Elderly

What the below rules boil down to is that when evaluating disability in individuals age 65 or older, the older the individual, the more likely it is that they will be determined to be disabled, with little or no scrutiny. Here is an excerpt from the SSA ruling on the subject:

> In general, the regulations and procedures for determining disability for adults under title XVI of the [Social Security] Act who are under age 65 are used when determining whether an individual age 65 or older is disabled.

> Adjudicators are required to consider any impairment(s) the individual has, including those that are often found in older individuals.

> If an individual age 72 or older has a medically determinable impairment, that impairment will be considered to be "severe."

> If the individual's impairment(s) prevents the performance of his or her past relevant work (PRW), or, if the individual does not have PRW, the adjudicator must consider two special medical-vocational profiles showing an inability to make an adjustment to other work . .

Generally, adjudicators should use the rules for individuals age 60-64 when determining whether an individual age 65 or older can perform other work.

Beginning at age 65, age is considered to be a factor that imposes greater limits on vocational adaptability for individuals who retain the functional capacity to perform medium work. If illiteracy in English or the inability to communicate in English further limits such an individual's vocational scope, a finding of "disabled" is warranted unless the individual's PRW was skilled or semiskilled and provided the individual with transferable skills.

Some individuals age 65 or older may not understand, or be able to comply with, our requests to submit evidence or attend a consultative examination (CE). Therefore, adjudicators must make special efforts in situations in which it appears that an individual age 65 or older may not be cooperating.

 The text can be read here:
http://www.ssa.gov/OP_Home/rulings/ssi/02/SSR99-03-ssi-02.html

Becoming Certified as Disabled

It can take a long time to become certified as disabled, generally six months. The examination and the screening are thorough.

The screening is based on qualifying younger people as disabled. Caseworkers often do not know that it is much more simple for an elderly person to be certified as disabled. The rules state that after age 65, and even more so after age 72, most people can be considered disabled on account of age.

⮕ If you are in great need of the benefits and the delay is causing you difficulties, one way to shorten the lengthy assessment period is to appeal even before the 6 months are up. The judge will often give a ruling in your favor because the lengthy assessment is not generally required of elderly disabled people.

You may have to prove that you became disabled after arriving in the U.S. You can cite the results of the medical examination you underwent during the immigration procedure. This is weak evidence, but it may be sufficient.

Difference Between Disability Under SS and SSI

If you are under 65, and you are working and are fully insured, and become disabled, then you can get disability under either Social Security or SSI. There are differences between the two programs that you should consider before applying.

Disability under Social Security

If you apply for disability through Social Security, your resources and income are not counted.

However, you receive no benefits for 5 months (then you receive the benefits retroactively). Perhaps more importantly, you do not receive Medicare benefits for 18 months after you are certified as disabled. (And one assumes you do not qualify for Medi-Cal because of your resources.)

Disability under SSI

You can apply for SSI even if you are working. You must be eligible for SSI based on your immigration status and your resources. (See "Spending Down Rules" on page 88 for some legitimate ways you can reduce your resources.)

The advantage of this program are that you do not have to wait for 5 months before you begin to receive benefits, and you can immediately receive Medi-Cal.

Eligibility for CAPI

 Go to http://www.nilc.org/ciwc/ciwc_ce/CAPI.htm for a good summary.

The state of California Cash Assistance Program for Immigrants (CAPI) program aims to meet the needs of qualified immigrants who would otherwise be eligible for SSI but are not eligible because of their immigrant status.

CAPI uses the same eligibility rules as SSI, and mostly uses the same deeming rules. As a non-citizen and a legal immigrant, you are eligible for CAPI only if you meet the SSI income and resources criteria but are not eligible because of your immigration status – and you fall in any of these categories:

- You are a pre 8/22/96 entrant. Such entrants were eligible after the 3-year deeming period. This affects only those who were not eligible for SSI before 8/22/96, or at the current time.
- You are a post 8/22/96 entrant, but you signed the traditional affidavit (which was used through 1997) and you became disabled after arriving in the U.S, and the 3-year sponsor deeming period is complete (which, of course, it is by now).
- You are a post-8/22/96 entrant, you signed the new deeming agreement, and the 10-year CAPI deeming period is complete.

- You are a post-8/22/96 entrant, you signed the new deeming agreement, and the 10-year CAPI deeming period is NOT complete, but your sponsor has become disabled.
- You are a post-8/22/96 entrant, you signed the new deeming agreement, and the 10-year CAPI deeming period is NOT complete, but your sponsor or sponsor's spouse is abusive.
- You would go hungry or be homeless without this benefit.

If you are disabled and otherwise eligible for CAPI, agency officers may disregard the sponsor deeming on a discretionary basis, especially if you have completed 5 years residency. The rules are complex.

> You are considered likely to go "hungry or homeless" if the income you actually receive is less than the federal SSI benefit rate. This exception does not apply if you receive free room and board.

Age-Out Protection for Minor Immigrants

President Bush on August 6th 2002 signed the Child Status Protection Act. This new Law addresses the problem of minor children losing their eligibility for certain immigration benefits as a result of BCIS processing delays.

Prior to the passage of this Law, child eligibility to receive a visa or to be part of his or her parent's application was based on the child's age at the time that the alien relative petition was approved, not the time the petition was filed.

Because of enormous backlogs and processing delays many children turned 21 before the BCIS (then called the INS) adjudicated the petition. In such cases the child " aged-out" and was ineligible to receive an immediate relative visa or was no longer considered to be part of the parent's application. The child's petition was either automatically moved to a lower preference category or the child was required to submit his or her own petition, resulting in years of delays and possible ineligibility.

The Act provides that the determination whether an unmarried alien or daughter of a US citizen is considered an *immediate relative child* (under 21 years of age) is based on the age of the alien at the time the petition for alien relative (Form 1-130) is filed on his or her behalf rather than on the date the petition is adjudicated as was the case under the prior law.

The Law makes similar determinations in the case of permanent resident parents who subsequently naturalize after having filed petitions for their sons or daughters, and citizen parents who filed petitions for married sons or daughters where sons and daughters later divorce. In the former case, the age determination will be made at the time of the parent's naturalization. In the latter the Alien beneficiary's age will be determined as if the date of his or her divorce.

For the children of legal permanent residents, or those who are accompanying or following to join on a petition for an immigrant visa; their eligibility will be determined based on the date that a visa becomes available to them but only if they seek to acquire permanent resident status within one year of such availability.

In addition the new Law provides age-out protection to alien children who accompany or follow to join parents who have filed for asylum or refugee status.

Finally the new law provides that the family sponsored petition of an unmarried alien son or daughter whose permanent resident parent subsequently becomes a naturalized Us citizen will be converted to a petition for an unmarried son or daughter of a US citizen, unless the son or daughter elects otherwise.

Deeming Period Rules in California

Under the deeming rules, the income and resources of an immigrant's sponsor (and the sponsor's spouse) are added to those of the immigrant in determining the immigrant's eligibility for benefits. Deeming rules often render an immigrant "over income" for a benefit, but if the sponsor income is very low, the immigrant may still qualify.

The deeming rules used depend partly on whether the immigrant's sponsor signed the "traditional" affidavit of support (INS form I –134) or the "new" affidavit of support (INS form I-864). The new affidavits of support went into use on December 19, 1997 as a provision of the Immigration Act.

Some immigrants who entered the U.S. after that date have an old affidavit on file and that affidavit is used for deeming purposes.

 Go to http://policy.ssa.gov/poms.nsf/lnx/0500502200 for the official explanation of the old and new sponsor deeming rules.

Deeming generally does not apply to immigrants who are required to have an affidavit of support on file, e.g., refugees, asylees, parolees, and battered spouses or children who file a "self-petition" for an immigrant visa.

Table 1 Eligibility for Major Benefits Program in California

| | Qualified Immigrants[1] | | Not Qualified Immigrants[2] |
	Entered U.S Before Aug 22, 1996	Entered U.S On or After Aug 22, 1996	
SSI/ SSP	Receiving SSI (or application pending) on Aug. 22, 1996 Qualified as disabled[3*] Veteran, active duty military, their spouse, un-remarried surviving spouse, or child[*] Lawful permanent resident with credit for 40 quarters of work[4*] Refugee, asylees, granted withholding of deportation, Cuban/ Haitian entrant, Amerasian, *but only during first 7 years after getting status* American Indian born in Canada or other Native American tribal member born outside U.S.	Veteran, active duty military, their spouse, un-remarried surviving spouse, or child[*] Lawful permanent resident with credit for 40 quarters of work[4*] (but must wait until 5 years after entry before applying) Refugee, asylees, granted withholding of deportation, Cuban/ Haitian entrant, Amerasian, *but only during first 7 years after getting status* American Indian born in Canada or other Native American tribal member born outside U.S.	Receiving SSI (or application pending) on Aug. 22, 1996 American Indian born in Canada or other Native American tribal member born outside U.S.
CAPI	Are 65 years or older[5] but do not meet Immigrant eligibility criteria for federal SSI (above) *	Are 65 years or older or a person with disabilities, but do not meet Immigrant eligibility criteria for federal SSI (above) *	Are permanently residing in the U.S. under color of law (PRUCOL), and are 65 or older or a person with disabilities

[1] **Qualified Immigrants** are (1) lawful permanent residents (LPRs), Including Amerasian immigrants; (2) refugees, asylees, persons granted withholding of deportation, conditional entry (In effect prior to Apr. 1, 1980), or paroled for at least one year; (3) Cuban/ Haitian entrants; and (4) battered spouses and

children with a pending or approved (a) self-petition for an immigrant visa, or (b) immigrant visa filed for a spouse or child by a U.S citizen or LPR, or (c) application for cancellation of removal/ suspension of deportation, whose need for benefits has a substantial connection to the battery or cruelty. Parent/ child of such battered child/ spouse are also qualified. Victims of trafficking (who are not included in the "qualified" immigrant definition) are eligible for all benefits funded or administered by federal agencies, without regard to their immigration status.

[2] **Not qualified immigrants** include all non-citizens who do not fit within the "qualified immigrant" categories.

[3] Must have been lawfully residing in the U.S. on Aug 22, 1996

[4] LPRs can earn credit if they have worked 40 qualifying quarters. Immigrants also get credits towards their 40 quarters for work performed: (1) by parents when the immigrant was under 18; and (2) by spouse during the marriage (unless marriage ended in divorce or annulment). No credit is given for quarter worked after Dec. 3, 1996 if a federal means-tested benefits (SSI, Medi-Cal, food stamps, Cal Works or Healthy Families was received in that quarter.

[5] Qualified immigrants with disabilities, who were not lawfully present in the U.S on Aug. 22, 1996, are also eligible for CAPI.

During the deeming period, a sponsor's income/ resource may be added to the immigrant's in determining eligibility. See Table 2.

Table 2 Deeming Periods for Traditional and New Affidavits

		CalWorks	Food Stamps		CAPI	SSI
			State	**Federal**		
Traditional Affidavit	**Deeming**	No deeming	No deeming	No deeming	3 yrs for pre 8/22/96 entrants; else 10 years or 3 yrs if sponsor disabled	3 Years
	Exemptions	N/A	N/A	N/A	Become blind or disabled after entry Domestic Violence victim	Become blind or disabled after entry
New Affidavit	**Deeming**	Until citizenship or 40 Credits	3 Years	Until citizenship or 40 Credits	10 Years	Until citizenship or 40 Credits
	Exemptions	Would go hungry or homeless without benefits[3] Domestic violence victim[4]	Would go hungry or homeless without benefits[3] Domestic violence victim (no time limit) Sponsor in the same food stamp household	Would go hungry or homeless without benefits[3] Domestic violence victim[4]	Would go hungry or homeless without benefits[3] Domestic violence victim (no time limit)	Would go hungry or homeless without benefits[3] Domestic violence victim[4]

---

[3] 12 months
[4] 12 months or longer if abuse recognized by INS, ALJ, or a court.

Chapter 4
More Important Highlights

This chapter highlights some important general points that apply to any welfare applicant. It contains sections on the following:

The Importance of Reporting Honestly

As the Chinese wise men say, **if you don't want anybody to know it, don't do it,**

You must give a full account of all your income and resources in any part of the world when applying for welfare. Some resources are exempt, for example those you cannot liquidate for legal reasons. However, you must report them all.

⮡ You must report any changes in your living conditions within 10 days, especially when the changes are likely to have any effect on eligibility for SSI.

Interchange of information between SSA, BCIS, IRS

The Welfare Reform act includes these provisions:

* Federal and State entities are required to notify the Bureau of Citizenship and Immigration Services (BCIS, formerly known as the Immigration and Naturalization Service or INS) of any non-citizen that the entity *knows* is not lawfully present in the U.S.

* Similarly the Agency, later on, may make use of available technology and find out details of the income and resources of the welfare claimant/recipient not only in USA but also in any part of the world.

* SSA has published notice that it will begin computer matching with the IRS to identify sources and amounts of unearned income reported to the IRS by SSI applicants and beneficiaries.

SSA Can Reopen and Revise a Decision

An SSI determination or decision is binding unless an appropriate appeal is filed within the required time period or it is subsequently reopened and revised. If the Social Security Administration finds good cause for reopening the case (that is, making an appeal) it can do it:

* Within twelve months of the date of the notice of the initial determination for any reason

* Within two years of the date of the notice of the initial determination, if the Agency finds *Good Cause* for reopening the case

* At any time, if the decision was obtained by fraud or similar fault

Similar Fault

There may not be any intention to defraud but if it is established that the recipient knowingly did something wrong, the Social Security Agency can determine what is known as *similar fault* and reopen a prior SSI determination. Though not frequently used, it is available. The definition of "similar fault" is given as follows on an SSA web site:

"Similar fault" exists when an SSI recipient or other person knowingly makes an incorrect or incomplete statement that is material to the determination for SSI payments or knowingly conceals information that is material to the determination of eligibility or amount of SSI payments. It differs from fraud in that fraudulent intent is not required. Unlike fraud, the *intent* to wrongfully procure (or increase) benefits need not be established."

 www.ssa.gov/OP_Home/rulings/ssi/07/SSR85-23-ssi-07.html

Penalties

If you do not comply honestly with the requirements of the SSA, you will be penalized.

Penalty of Non-Payment for False or Misleading Statements

The Foster Care Independence Act (December 14 1999) added a new penalty of non-payment of SSA/SSI benefits for individuals found to have knowingly made a false or misleading statement or to have omitted a material fact for use in determining eligibility. The new statutory provision applies to statements made on or after December 14, 1999.

The period of non-payment is 6 months for the first incident, 12 months for the second, and 24 months for the third or subsequent incident.

Congress passed this provision to penalize individuals who have provided false or misleading information to the SSA in order to qualify for benefits. However it is provided that Medi-Cal and Medicare benefits are not affected:

If benefits are lost under this provision, the affected individuals retain their right to Medicaid or Medicare benefits. Further, penalized individuals have a right to appeal adverse decisions.

It is therefore necessary to consult the Agency as to how best the loss can be reduced to the minimum.

Penalties for Not Reporting a Change

If you do not report an event that affects your SSI benefits (see next), there may be a penalty deduction in later benefit payments as follows:

- $ 25 penalty for first time
- $ 50 penalty for the second time
- $ 100 penalty for each subsequent failure

The penalty is not imposed if you were without fault or had a good cause for not reporting an event.

How to Obtain Your Records

Because of the Freedom of Information act, your records are all available to you. The Social Security Administration (SSA) must provide information requested by benefit claimants/recipients.

But you must be specific in your request. The SSA does not honor a request for "all my information."

You must be able to identify yourself in order to receive your records. You can make a request in person at an SSA office, or send a request my mail to the Manager of the office.

Right of Appeal

If you disagree with a decision made by the SSI agency, you have a right of appeal.

Contacting Your Congressperson

When to Go to Your Congressperson

When all else fails, if the SSA is denying you benefits for which you are sure you are eligible, you can appeal to the congressperson for your district. Your congressperson will act on your behalf. The SSA will "flag" your folder indicating there is a Congressional inquiry into your case.

Who is my U.S. Representative?

You can look up your congressperson (your representative in the US House of Representatives) on-line.

> Go to www.house.gov/writerep/ and enter your zip code. You can also send a message at this site.

Go to the House member web site lookup page at
www.house.gov/house/MemberWWW.html

How to Write a Letter to Your Congressperson

Here is an acceptable format for writing a letter to your congressperson. Replace the italic text and parentheses with your own information:

The Honorable Rep. (*fill in full name and check spelling*)
United States House of Representatives
Washington D.C. 20515
Dear Representative (*last name only*)

[*Letter….*]

If I may be of any help, or provide you with any further information, please do not hesitate to contact me. Thank you for your time.
Sincerely,
you…..
and your phone number, email address, and address.

Living Arrangement Guidelines

How you describe your living arrangements has a crucial impact on the SSA's determination of your eligibility for benefits, as well as the amount of benefits if you are eligible for welfare. For SSI, for example, your living arrangements can determine whether you will receive the full Federal benefit payment or a **one-third reduction**.

In-kind assistance likewise affects your eligibility and level of benefit. This section describes living arrangements, and the next deals with in-kind assistance.

⤳ The detailed rules are explained in Chapter 7, SSI Rules, on page 76. This section provides some guidelines that will help you understand the importance of the various rules.

In many cases referred to me, SSI recipients suffer a loss of one-third of their SSI benefit because they are unable to pay the *pro rata* share of the total expenditure of the household. This section has some guidelines that can help you avoid this situation.

It has also been reported to me that in many cases children with whom elderly parents live do not like to fill in the application form. It is embarrassing to admit that they charge their parents, from whom they received free board and lodging when they were young. Moreover they must show the payment as income in their tax returns. Because of this, many agencies do not insist on the form and rely instead on the claimant's oral or written statement. This can have consequences during an appeal.

Documentation is very helpful in supporting your case. Be sure to keep receipts for all expenses.

⤳ Many seniors have a joint account with their children. According to the rules, funds in such accounts are considered the funds of the person on SSI. SSI advises you to avoid doing this.

How Living Arrangements Affect SSI

The amount of your SSI benefit depends on whether you are paying for your food, shelter, and clothing, or whether someone else pays part or all of that expense (as explained in Chapter 7, SSI Rules, on page 76).

The impact of in-kind assistance and support given to you by others depends on whether it is used for food, clothing, and shelter or not. If the assistance is for food, clothing, and shelter (or some expense in this category) then it counts as income and affects your SSI eligibility. If it is for other basic expenses, and you cannot turn the gift into cash, it does not count.

If the in-kind support is for food, clothing, or shelter (or all three), then the impact on your SSI depends on your living arrangement.

Your living arrangement determines which of two rules is used to determine the effect of in-kind support and maintenance on your SSI: the Presumed Maximum Value (PMV) rule or the One Third Reduction rule (VTR). It is generally better to have a living arrangement that allows the Presumed Maximum Value (PMV) rule to be used.

The One Third Reduction rule applies if you live in another's household and receive BOTH food and shelter from them. Under this rule, if you don't pay the full pro rata share, you lose one third of your benefit – even if you are contributing *almost* the pro rata share.

In most other cases, the Presumed Maximum Value rule is used. Under this rule, you lose only the amount of the contribution that others make towards your support and maintenance. So if your family pays for $30 of your groceries, you lose $30 of your grant.

"In-Kind" Assistance Guidelines

⮑ The detailed rules are explained in Chapter 7, SSI Rules, on page 76. This section provides some guidelines that will help you understand the importance of the various rules.

You may be fortunate enough to receive some financial assistance from your family, whether in cash or in kind. Depending on the nature of the assistance, and what it is used for, this can affect your SSI eligibility (and hence your Medi-Cal eligibility) and the amount of your SSI grant. (See also Living Arrangement Guidelines above).

Cash you receive always counts as income. However, not all "in-kind" help counts as income as explained next.

Assistance With Food, Shelter, and Clothing Counts

In-kind assistance with expenses for food, shelter, and clothing counts as in-kind income. The consequence may be that you no longer meet the pro rata share of household expenses, and you may thus lose one third of your SSI grant. In kind support can reduce your benefits but cannot make you ineligible for benefits.

Even if you pay for most of your expenses, you are considered to be receiving free food and board if you don't meet the pro-rata share threshold (see "Paying a Pro Rata Share of Household Expenses" on page 93 for details).

⮑ In-kind support and maintenance is called "ISM" for short, in the government literature and web sites.

Assistance That Does Not Count

If you receive something that does *not* help with food, shelter or clothing, and which you *cannot convert to cash*, this does not count as income and also does not affect the pro rata share of household expenses.

⮑ If a family member wants to help you, ask them to pay for expenses other than your mortgage, property tax, property insurance, rent, food, clothing, or utilities.

Examples of gifts that do not count include payments made directly for car payments, gas and oil, auto insurance, car registration fees, veterinarian bills, cable television, magazine and newspapers, taxi script, and medical costs, including supplemental payment to an in-home support service (IHSS) provider.

If you can cash-in the gift, then the cash-in value is counted as income. If you receive something allowed as an exempt resource, such as an automobile, it does not count as an income when you receive it.

Subsidized Rent Usually Counts as Income

If you pay subsidized rent, which may be the case if you are renting from a relative, the difference between the rent you pay and the current market rent rate is counted as your income and therefore reduces your SSI grant or may make you ineligible.

When Rent Subsidy Doesn't Count as Income

In some cases, a rent that is lower than the current market rent is not considered as in-kind income when calculating SSI eligibility or benefits. For example:

- If you do work in exchange for a rent reduction, as long as the value of the in-kind income from the rent reduction is $65-85 per month or less.

- If there are economic reasons for the reduction. For example, the relative who rents you the space may be storing things there, or only wants one person in the room or apartment so it won't be torn up, or wants someone in the building who is home all day, or is thinking of selling and does not want someone in the apartment who would be difficult to get out.

- If the rent you pay is so high a proportion of your total income that it "flies in the face of reality" to think of any subsidy as in-kind income you could benefit from.

When the Rent is a High Proportion of Your Total Income

The United States Court of Appeals for the second circuit held that although the statute and regulations concerning in-kind income and rental subsidy are facially valid, if the *proportion of income* that an SSI recipient pays for housing is so great that it flies in the face of reality to conclude that unearned income in the form of housing subsidy is actually available to the recipient, the unearned income should be disregarded.

For example, if the market rent is $800, and you pay a big slice of your SSI towards rent, but not $800, the subsidy is not considered an economic benefit to you.

So – if you are not paying the pro rata (proportionate) share, but the amount you pay is a large proportion of your benefit, you can rebut any denial of benefits by saying the proportionate share "flies in the face of reality."

How Loans Affect Your SSI

A loan received for payment of food, clothing, and shelter will not be counted against an individual as his income. However, the SSA is likely to question how the loan is to be repaid. Provide full documentation to eliminate doubt about the genuine nature of the transaction.

⮚ The claimant may borrow funds (even from the head of household) to pay the pro-rata share and repay them later on, if the claimant can prove that he or she is expecting funds at some future date, for example, from sale of property or repatriation of rupees.

Applicants for SSI Disability Who Take a Loan

When you apply for SSI disability, you may not be in a financial position to pay for food and shelter. Your relative or friend may help you out with a loan. You must make it clear that you intend to repay this loan, and that you intend to pay for your food, shelter, and clothing from the SSI you will receive. In the case of retrospective payment of SSI, say after 5 months, the food and shelter expenses for all the five months can be paid back to your creditor from the arrears of SSI. The position should be made clear at the time of application.

Summary of Advice

* If you are eligible for SSI, you are eligible for Medi-Cal. It is important to maintain your SSI eligibility for this reason alone!
* In-kind support that you receive can reduce benefits for SSI (and Medi-Cal) but it cannot make you ineligible for benefits.
* Pay for your own rent, food, and clothing from whatever you get as SSI. If you cannot meet other expenses, and a family member wishes to help, ask them to directly pay for those expenses, for example, telephone bills, automobile expenses, club fees, books and magazines, and so on.

- Keep all receipts as documentation in case you wish to make an appeal against benefit reductions.
- It may be possible for you to change your living arrangement so the PMV rule applies to you, instead of the VTR rule.

Keep your Medi-Cal Coverage

Selling Real Estate?

You are allowed up to 9 months to sell real estate. During this selling period, the property is excluded from your resources, for calculating SSI and Medi-Cal benefits. Benefits given during this period are known as "conditional benefits."

Even after 9 months, if you can prove that you are making reasonable efforts to sell the property but it is not selling, the property can still be excluded for as long as you continue to make reasonable efforts to sell it. The SSA will request evidence every three months that you are in fact still trying to sell the property.

If the property sells within 9 months, you must then repay the SSI benefits received during the 9-month period (or however many months it takes to sell the property within that period), because the benefits are then considered to be an *overpayment*.

If the property takes longer than 9 months to sell, you repay only 9 months SSI benefits. Benefits paid after the 9-month period are NOT considered to be overpayment when the property finally sells. The benefits are *not* conditional during this period.

If the property doesn't sell at all, you don't have to repay any benefits.

However, regardless of when the property sells, you do NOT have to repay any money for Medi-Cal coverage. It is very important to keep your health insurance, and there is no reason for you not to be covered in this case.

Medi-Cal and Non-Cash Resources

In general, if you have any resources that cannot be easily converted to cash, they are generally not counted for Medi-Cal, even if they are counted for SSI. This is because you cannot pay medical bills with non-cash resources.

Craig V. Bonta: Keeping Medi-Cal When Benefits are Stopped

Some people have Medi-Cal coverage because they are eligible for another program such as SSI. In the past, if the other program was stopped, for example because the recipient was no longer eligible, Medi-Cal would also be stopped automatically. This caused great hardship. Today, this should not happen, but not all caseworkers are aware of the change. If it happens to you, cite "Craig v. Bonta" to your caseworker or appeals judge.

As a result of the Craig v. Bonta case, the provisions of Senate Bill (SB) 87 now cover those who have Medi-Cal through another program. SB 87 states that DHS must review the case and investigate whether the recipient might be eligible for Medi-Cal on some other basis. They must also attempt to contact the person by phone, and send them a "request for information" form.

Chapter 5
A Summary of Social Insurance Benefits

Go to www.ssa.gov for more information. This government web site provides comprehensive information about SSA, including Social Security, SSI, disability benefits, and Medicaid.

This chapter contains sections on the following:

Social Security

The Social Security Act was passed in 1935. The system consisted of measures designed to give some financial protection or security to those who retire from work either due to old age or disability. The relief was also to be given to their families, dependents and survivors.

The Social Security Act provides for benefit payments of different kinds to many people. Each type of benefit has specific eligibility requirements. The Act now covers about 96% of the American work force. During the year 2000, more than 45 million people received cash benefits at a rate exceeding $34 billion each month.

The Social Security Administration warns Americans "Social Security is not intended to be your only source of income." Instead, it is to be used as a supplement to pensions, insurance, savings and other investments one accumulates during working years.

 Go to www.socialsecurity.gov/OP_Home for details of many rules and regulations governing Social Security, including the Compilation of the Social Security Laws, the Code of Federal Regulations, the Social Security Handbook, and Social Security rulings.

Social Security and Medicare Tax

Every time a worker receives a paycheck, part of her or his wages is deducted and paid into the system. At the same time, the employer is required to make an equal payment on the worker's behalf. When the workers retire they, their families and dependents, as well as their survivors after their death receive small payments from the program.

The compulsory contributions are treated as a tax, called the Social Security tax. Contributions are not exactly matched with the amount of benefits paid. However benefits are paid as an earned right. No means test is imposed. There is no stigma attached to it.

Social Security tax is 6.2%. Medicare (hospital insurance) tax is 1.45%. Self-employed persons pay double – that is, 15.30% of their earnings.

Tax is not levied on annual earnings over $87,000 (2003). There is no limit for Medicare Tax.

Entitlement to Benefits

Insured Status is Based on Credits

 Go to www.ssa.gov/pubs/10072.html for detailed and current information about credits.

Anyone who has obtained *Insured Status* is entitled to receive Social Security benefits. To become eligible for Social Security benefits, a worker must earn a minimum number of credits based on work in covered employment, or in self-employment.

Social Security credits were known earlier as quarters of coverage. Now the credits are determined by amount earned in a year.

The amount of earnings required per credit is adjusted automatically each year in proportion to increases in the average wage level. In 2003, a credit is given for each $890 in annual covered earnings, up to a maximum of four credits for the year.

In other words, earnings of $3,560 or more in 2003 will give the worker four credits, regardless of when the money is actually earned or paid during the year.

Requirements to be Considered Fully Insured

To be eligible for most types of benefits, such as retirement benefits, the worker must be *fully insured*. To be fully insured the worker must have a certain number of credits.

* Anyone who turns 62 in 1991 or earlier needs 40 credits to be fully insured.
* People who turn 62 after 1991 need a few more credits.
* People born before 1929 need fewer credits.

It is not the number of credits that determines your monthly payment. It is your average earnings over your working years that determine how much your monthly payment will be.

Combining Credits for SSI Eligibility

You and your spouse can combine credits to achieve the 40-credit threshold, and then you may be eligible for SSI (generally after you have been a qualified alien for 5 years). For example, if you have 22 and your spouse has 20, you have 42 credits combined. Since your SS benefit may be small, you may be eligible for SSI. This is explained in Chapter 3, Highlights for Immigrants – See "Combining Credits" on page 27 for details.

If You or Your Family Receives Federal Means-tested Benefits

For the purpose of counting credits for SSI eligibility, the following additional rule applies. After December 31, 1996, no credits are awarded for any period in which an individual receives any Federal means-tested public benefit, including any SSI. This rule also applies if the individual's spouse, or dependent children receive such benefits. This does not apply to counting credits for Social Security eligibility.

> Note that Medi-Cal is not a Federal benefit or considered a public charge, and does not affect credits awarded.

Eligibility for Benefits if you are Not Fully Insured

Many immigrants have not been in the country long enough to earn 40 credits. Some benefits are still available for those with some credits.

> Immigrants with 40 qualifying credits are eligible for SSI after the 5-year deeming period.

For workers who become disabled or die before age 62, the number of credits necessary for fully insured status depends on their age at the time they become disabled or die. A minimum of 6 credits is required regardless of age.

Those who die or become disabled before they are fully insured are eligible for survivor or disability benefits.

If a worker dies before achieving fully insured status, benefits can still be paid to qualified survivors if the worker was "currently insured" at the time of death. To be currently insured the worker must have earned 6 credits during the 12 quarters before death.

Payment of Social Security Benefits

Payment normally begins after the insured person has reached full retirement age.

Full Retirement Age

Full retirement age depends on your birth date. It is 65 for those born before 1938, and 67 for those born after 1960. For those born in between those years, full retirement age gradually increases. For example, for those born in 1955, full retirement age is 66 years and 2 months.

 Go to www.ssa.gov/retirechartred.htm for complete details about full retirement age.

Early Retirement

Once workers have attained fully insured status, they may opt for retirement at age 62 but their benefits are reduced, for the remainder of their life. The closer you are to retirement age, the less the benefit is reduced. But bear in mind, that this reduction is permanent.

Working During Retirement

The Senior Citizen's Freedom to Work Act of 2000, effective January 1, 2000, eliminated the retirement earnings test for persons who have attained full retirement age. That is, if you have attained full retirement age, there is no restriction on your earnings. (Formerly you lost one dollar of benefit out of three.)

People who collect Social Security before the year in which they reach full retirement age will lose one dollar of those benefits for every two dollars they earn over a set yearly limit. For the year 2003, the limit is $11,520. The limit applies only to earnings from work and not to income from savings, investments, pensions, rental property, and so on.

In the year in which you reach full retirement age a different rule applies. During the months of that year that are prior to your birthday, you will lose one dollar of benefits for every three dollars you earn over a set yearly limit. For the year 2003, that limit is

$30,720 (only counting earnings in the months prior to your birthday). After your birthday, you can earn any amount of money without losing benefits.

 Source: Nolo Law for All, Retirement and Elder Care: http://www.nolo.com/lawcenter/ency/index.cfm/catID/84404409-3882-4800-81764383AA66993B

Unemployment Programs

Through federal and state cooperation, unemployment programs are designed to provide benefits to regularly employed members of the labor force who become un-voluntarily unemployed and who are willing and able to accept suitable employment.

To pay for these benefits, a uniform Federal tax is imposed on the payrolls of industrial and commercial worker's employers who employ eight or more workers for 20 or more weeks in a calendar year. Some states also levy a payroll tax.

Contributions collected from employers are deposited in separate Federal Trust Funds for each state. States are given grants to administer the Federal programs using these funds, and must meet certain Federal requirements. The state decides the amount and duration of benefits. Almost all workplaces are required to pay payroll taxes and their employees will get benefits.

Entitlement and Payment

Unemployment benefits are available as a matter of right and are not means tested. They are paid on a weekly basis and are generally 50% of wages. Some states provide additional allowance for dependents. Generally a waiting period of a week after becoming unemployed is required. Generally, benefits are given for 26 weeks and the benefits may be extended for 13 more weeks.

After you get work (or otherwise go off the unemployment benefit program), if you are again made unemployed, you must wait for 13 weeks to become eligible for unemployment benefits again.

Disability Insurance

Disability Insurance is a Federal program established in 1956. Three different kinds of social security benefits are paid on account of disability:

* Disability Insurance benefit
* Disabled Child benefit
* Disabled Widow benefit

The most common and well known is the Disability Insurance benefit. The amount of the benefit is the same as if the worker has reached the age of retirement.

You may not consider yourself disabled, and yet, by the government definition, you might be. (See "The SSA Definition of Disability" on page 30 for details.) Do not decide for yourself whether you are eligible for disability benefits. Use the government definition, given above, and apply to get a medical examination so that a doctor can make the objective determination of your ability to work.

Eligibility Requirements

To qualify for disability benefits, workers must meet the following conditions:

* Their age must be less than full retirement age. (For those over sixty-five, other benefits are provided in the case of disability).
* They must have recent work activity: if over 31, they must have at least 20 credits, earned in the 10 years before the disability began. If born after 1977, six credits are required, earned in the three years before the disability began. (The recent work requirement does not apply to blind people.)
* They must have enough Social Insurance credits to be considered fully insured.

⊃ Caseworkers do not always realize that people over retirement age who do *not* qualify for social insurance benefits *are* eligible for disability benefits through SSI if they are otherwise eligible. See "Disability and Eligibility for SSI" on page 28, for information on disability benefits that may apply to you.

Benefits for Dependents

Dependents are a spouse and child or children. They are also covered by a worker's disability benefits. The rate of payment depends upon the worker's annual earnings at the time of retirement and age at retirement. (See the section "Full Retirement Age" on page 59 for details about the effect of age at retirement.)

Dependents get half the benefits for which the worker is eligible.

A spouse is eligible to receive benefits at any age if caring for a child who is under 16 or who is disabled and under 22. Otherwise the spouse is eligible after reaching the age of 62.

Unmarried children are eligible to receive benefits if they are under age 18, or up to 19 if in high school, or disabled before age 22.

Five Months Waiting Period and Retroactive Payment

The disability benefit has a waiting period of 5 months. Disability must be certified during the entire 5 months. During the waiting period, benefits are not paid. However, the benefits for this waiting period are paid after the waiting period is up, if the person is still disabled.

Disability benefits may be paid retroactively up to 12 months, not including the waiting period. Totally, then, retroactive payments are available for up to 17 months after the disability begins.

Temporary Total Disability

In the case of Temporary Total Disability, workers are unable to work during recovery period but are expected to recover.

If workers are unable to work for more than the five months waiting period they get two-thirds of their wages, or more if the wages are low. In some cases workers get permanent disability benefits.

Permanent Partial Disability, Death Benefits, and Medical Benefits

Permanent Partial Disability, Death Benefits and Medical Benefits are payable. In the case of private employment, the benefits are payable by the employers. Employers may provide disability insurance privately, to safeguard their liabilities.

In some states the employers are not permitted to take private insurance. They have to insure with the State Fund. In some other states the states compete with private insurers.

Worker's Compensation

Worker's compensation was the first form of social insurance to develop widely in the United States. By an act of 1908, the Federal government applied it to its civilian employees engaged in hazardous task. The remaining federal work force was covered in 1916.

Today all 50 states including the District of Columbia are covered. Puerto Rico and Virgin Islands have their own program.

Worker's compensation provides cash benefits and medical care when employees suffer work-related injuries. The workers get benefits but in exchange they forfeit their right to sue the employers.

In 1999, State and Federal Worker's Compensation Laws covered about 123.9 million employees with a payment of $4.1 trillion. The program is compulsory for most private employers. In Texas it is elective but if the employer does not elect to admit compensation, the worker may go to the court and employers are debarred from alleging contributory negligence on the part of the worker.

In addition to cash payment and medical services, death and funeral benefits are also provided.

Medicare

Go to www.medicare.gov for more information on Medicare.

Medicare was established in 1965. It is a health insurance program for those 65 and older and some disabled people.

Total disbursement for Medicare in year 2000 was $222 billion and premium on tax receipts was less than that. The country is rightly worried about the solvency of the Medicare program.

The Medicare program covers 95% of the aged population, and people getting social security disability benefits.

Medicare consists of three parts:

* Hospital Insurance (HI), known as Part A
* Supplementary Medical Insurance (SMI), known as Part B
* Medicare plus Choice, known as Part C (established in 1997)

Parts A and B are also known as the Original Medicare Plan. Part C is an alternative to the Original Medicare Plan.

Because Medicare is such an important topic, it is covered in a separate chapter. See Chapter 8, Medicare and Medi-Cal , on page 104.

Earned Income Tax Credit (EITC)

 For current guidelines go to www.irs.gov/pub/irs-pdf/p596.pdf

The Earned Income Tax Credit program was established in 1975. It is a refundable tax credit that subsidizes wages of low-income workers. As it is tied to work, it is free from partisan attack. When the Republicans in the house wanted to delay EITC payments, (the first) President Bush went after them with vigor for trying to balance the budgets on the backs of the poor. President Clinton expanded it significantly in his first budget and in 2000 proposed another expansion.

This program is popular with employers, because it encourages workers to accept very low pay to get the benefit of the tax credit.

Income and family size determine the amount of the EITC. To qualify for the credit, both the earned income and the adjusted gross income for 2002 must be less than $29,201 for a taxpayer with one qualifying child ($30,201 for married filing jointly), $33,178 for a taxpayer with more than one qualifying child ($34,178 for married filing jointly), and $11,060 for a taxpayer with no qualifying children ($12,060 for married filing jointly).

The maximum credit for families with two or more children is around $4,100 for the 2002 tax year. The actual credit is calculated by the IRS based on the individual situation.

Even those who do not earn enough to pay taxes will receive this refund!

Temporary Disability Insurance

Temporary Disability Insurance has been established in only 5 states, Puerto Rico and the Railroad Industry.

This program partially compensates for the loss of wages caused by temporary non-occupational disability, or maternity.

The first state to establish the program was Rhode Island in 1942, California and the railroad in 1946, New Jersey in 1948 and New York in 1949, Puerto Rico in 1968 and Hawaii in 1969.

It covers commercial and industrial wage and salary workers. Principal occupational groups excluded are domestic workers, family workers, government employees and the self-employed.

The laws in each state are different for different workers. A worker must have a specified amount of past employment and must be disabled. All laws pay full benefit for pregnancy. Employees and employers both contribute.

Chapter 6
A Summary of Public Assistance Benefits

Public assistance is available to the elderly with limited income and resources who are not fully insured (and so do not get social security payments). The situation for immigrants is complex. Many benefits are not available until after the sponsor deeming period, and some are not available to non-citizens, with a few exceptions. This chapter summarizes the benefits and eligibility requirements. SSI and Medi-Cal are further explained in their own chapters. This chapter contains sections on the following:

- Supplemental Security Income (SSI), page 68
- Medicaid, page 70
- Food Stamps, page 70
- General Assistance, page 72
- Temporary Assistance for Needy Families (TANF), page 75

On-line Resources

Go to http://www.socialsecurity.gov/notices/supplemental-security-income for information on Federal public assistance benefits.

http://www.workworld.org/wwwebhelp.html has excellent summaries too.

Supplemental Security Income (SSI)

Supplemental Security Income, known as SSI, is a Federal income supplement program funded by general tax revenues. It was established under Public Law 92-603 on 30th October 1972 and came into effect on January 1, 1974.

SSI provides income support to persons aged 65 or older, as well as blind and disabled people of any age. It provides cash to meet basic needs for food, clothing, and shelter. It is a means-tested program and a program of last resort. The person applying must not have income and resources beyond a prescribed limit. The person must take all appropriate steps to get his legitimate dues from any other source before applying for SSI.

Immigrants and SSI

Most immigrants who arrived after the Welfare Reform Act of 1996 and who are non-citizens are not eligible for SSI, except for a minority of cases who meet certain requirements.

However, it is important to understand SSI rules, because many of them are also used to determine Medicaid eligibility. In addition, some elderly immigrants are eligible for SSI on the basis of disability.

Useful guidelines for immigrants are provided in "Eligibility for SSI" on page 25 and "Eligibility for CAPI" on page 26. SSI is covered in detail in Chapter 7, SSI Rules, on page 76.

Medicaid

Medicaid is a means-tested program established in 1965. It is a cooperative venture funded by both the Federal and State governments. It pays for medical assistance to certain individuals and families with low income and resources. Medicaid is the largest source of funding for medical and health-related services for America's poorest people. In California, Medicaid is called *Medi-Cal*. The State has been liberal so far. However, with the current budget shortfall, the future must be in question.

> Medi-Cal is covered in detail in Chapter 8, Medicare and Medi-Cal , on page 104.

Medicaid Benefits Vary from State to State

Medicaid is federally funded, but run at the State level. There are broad national guidelines for Medicaid. However, each State establishes its own eligibility standards, determines the types of services, sets the rate of payment for services and administers its own program. Because of this, a person who is eligible for Medicaid in one state may not be found eligible in another state. The services available in one state may not be available in other state.

Each state has the option of giving full medical services to immigrant seniors and disabled. Each state also has the option of refusing to provide these services. It is legitimate for states to refuse medical assistance to seniors and disabled people for five years after their arrival, if they entered the country on or after 22/8/96. California does not have an exclusion period. It also provides emergency-level medical services to immigrants who have not yet received their green card (they are PRUCOL immigrants at this stage).

State-Only Medical Programs

Most states also have a state-only program to provide medical assistance for specified poor persons who do not quality for Medicaid (borderline cases). For such services, the State does not get federal funds. Even some counties have additional services.

Food Stamps

 Go to www.fns.usda.gov/fsp/ for information about the Food Stamp program.

The Food Stamp program was established in 1977. It is a means-tested program administered nationally by the Food and Nutrition Service of the Department of Agriculture. In the fiscal year 2000, the average number of participants was 17.2 million and total benefits $15 billion. On Oct. 2, 2002, the Electronic Benefit Transfer (EBT) card was introduced.

Food stamps are as much a way of keeping the nation's farming, food processing and food sales industry solvent as they are of helping the poor. They create an important market for these industries.

The basic principle behind the program is a simple one. No one in America should be allowed to starve or become seriously malnourished and ill because he or she has not enough money to buy food.

Eligibility for the Food Stamp program and the amount of the benefits depend on income and size of household. Households without income receive full benefits; others, according to their income. An eligible four-person household with no income currently receives $465 per month in Food Stamps. This amount is updated every October.

All households in which all members receive Temporary Assistance for Needy Families (TANF) are categorically eligible for food stamps without regard to income or resources criteria.

Qualified Immigrants

There are different rules for "Qualified Immigrants" who entered the U.S. before August 22, 1996 and those who enter after that date. A legal permanent resident whose sponsor signed a new affidavit of support (I-864) is subject to deeming until she or he becomes a citizen or has 40 credits.

In California, those who get SSI are not eligible for food stamps while people on CAPI may get $10 a month. As the rules are complicated, those who need food stamps should obtain adequate information from the county disbursing the food stamps.

In California, immigrants who are otherwise eligible but do not meet the criteria for qualified immigrants may be covered by a more liberal State Food Stamps program.

General Assistance

General Assistance is a cash assistance program for adults. It is a kind of loan, repayable from any cash welfare received in future. Its duration is generally 60 months. The recipient has to be prepared to accept gainful work. People over 65 may be exempted from this requirement.

General Assistance is a county program, and continued payment is dependent upon the county's budget provision.

Among those *not* eligible for the program are:

- Those who are getting other forms of cash assistance.
- Those who have obtained their Green Card within the prior three years, unless they are eligible for any of the reasons listed next.

Among those eligible for this program (if they meet all other eligibility criteria) are:

- Children, including children born in the U.S. to undocumented aliens
- Adults who are victims of domestic violence
- Pregnant women
- People who take care of children below 19 years age
- PRUCOL residents

PRUCOL refers to the status of an undocumented alien permanently residing in the United States "under color of LAW" – that is to say, as if he is a documented alien. PRUCOL requires proof that the alien is residing with the knowledge and permission of the BCIS and that the BCIS does not contemplate deportation.)

In Santa Clara County, General Assistance is a part of the State of California CalWORKS program.

www.dss.cahwnet.gov/cdssweb/california_169.htm has for more information on the CalWORKS program.

Cash Assistance Program for Immigrants (CAPI)

The Cash Assistance Program for Immigrants is available only in the state of California. It is similar to SSI and follows all the same rules. It was meant to cover those who are not eligible for other benefits because of their immigration status, but who otherwise qualify for benefits.

For example, elderly, blind, and disabled immigrants whose condition began before 8/22/96 but who applied for SSI after that date, and who were not considered eligible because of their immigration status, are covered by CAPI.

See "Eligibility for CAPI" on page 33 for details.

Low Income Home Energy Assistance Program

The Low Income Home Energy Assistance program was started in 1981 and is managed by the Department of Health and Human Services Administration for Children and Families. Any individual or group of individuals living together as one economic unit in which residential energy is customarily purchased in common, either directly or through rent is eligible. There are income limits. However those who are in receipt of TANF, SSI, Food stamps, or needs-tested veterans benefits are eligible.

No household is excluded from eligibility on the basis of income alone if the household income is less than 110% of the poverty guidelines. The guidelines change over time. For a single person the poverty guideline is generally $8980, and for a couple, $12,120 (it can depend where you live, and it is reviewed every February). Expenditure for heating or cooling cost, and for home energy crises, is admissible. In 1999, for example, because of an extraordinary heat wave and floods, $1.1 billion were appropriated to provide extra relief.

Go to www.acf.dhhs.gov/programs/liheap/ for information about the LIHEAP program.

Go to http://aspe.hhs.gov/poverty/03poverty.htm for information about the poverty guidelines.

Temporary Assistance for Needy Families (TANF)

The Temporary Assistance for Needy Families (TANF) program was created in 1996 as a result of welfare reforms. It replaced the earlier program, Assistance to Families with Dependent Children (AFDC). The program is managed by the Department of Health and Human Services Administration for Children and Families. It is currently being assessed and may change in the near future.

The TANF program marks an end of federal entitlement to assistance. States and territories operate the program. It is a program requiring work in exchange for time-limited assistance.

The purpose of the program is to assist needy families so that children can be cared for in their homes. It is intended to reduce dependency of needy parents by promoting job preparation, work and marriage. It aims at preventing out-of-wedlock pregnancies and, it is intended to encourage the formation and maintenance of two-parent families.

 Go to www.acf.dhhs.gov/acf_services.html#walia for more information.

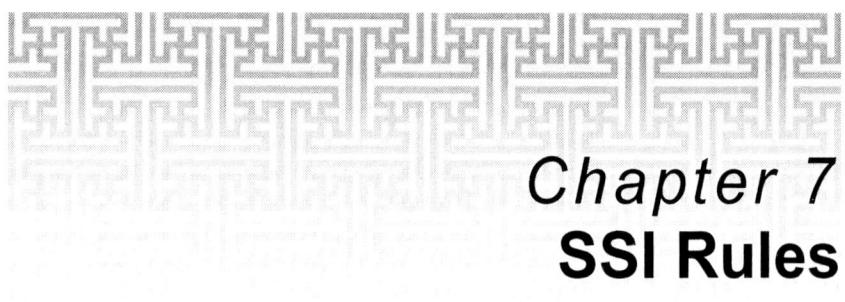

Chapter 7
SSI Rules

This chapter contains sections on the following:

Resources

On-line resources are a little tricky to find. Here are some useful ones:

- The main SSI page: www.socialsecurity.gov/notices/supplemental-security-income

- A very helpful online booklet called "Understanding Supplemental Security Income" is available at: http://www.socialsecurity.gov/notices/supplemental-security-income/text-understanding-ssi.htm

- Basic rules about who can get SSI: www.ssa.gov/pubs/11000.html

- Go to www.socialsecurity.gov/OP_Home/cfr20/416/416-0000.htm for a detailed explanation of the rules.

- Rules for non-citizens: www.ssa.gov/pubs/11051.html and also at http://www.socialsecurity.gov/notices/supplemental-security-income/spotlights/spot-non-citizens.htm

- Go to http://www.ssa.gov/pubs/11125.html for an explanation of SSI in California.

- Go to http://www.workworld.org/wwwebhelp/ssiget.htm for an excellent guide to SSI benefits and requirements.

Eligibility Rules

To qualify for SSI, the basic rule is that your monthly income minus exemptions must not be more than the current Federal Benefit Rate (FBR), or Federal Benefit Rate plus state supplement. California does have a state supplement. Additionally, those receiving SSI who return to work have higher income limits, as a Work Incentive. Your resources must also be within limits.

The amount of your SSI cash benefit will be the difference between your countable income and the FBR plus state supplement (see Maximum Benefit Rate, below).

Immigrant Eligibility for SSI

SSI is not available for many immigrants. See "Eligibility for SSI" on page 25 for eligibility rules for immigrants.

Even if you are Not Eligible Because of Immigrant Status

Even if you are not eligible for SSI because of your immigration status, it is important to understand SSI rules because they are often used in part to determine your eligibility for Medi-Cal benefits, which are explained in the next chapter.

Apply for Other Benefits First

SSI is a program of *last resort*. Therefore, before applying for SSI, a welfare claimant/recipient must first file for any other benefits for which he or she is eligible, such as Social Security, private pensions, and so on.

The Social Security Agency will provide you written notice of potential eligibility for other benefits and of your requirements to take "all appropriate steps" to pursue these benefits. You have thirty days from receipt of the notice to file for the benefits involved.

"Taking all appropriate steps" means:

- Applying for the benefit
- Providing any information necessary to establish eligibility

- Agreeing to receive the other benefits if you are found eligible

Even if the Agency does not provide you with this written notice, it is your duty to pursue other benefits yourself.

⮕ It is not required that you appeal denial of other benefits that you apply for. If you are denied all other benefits, you can then apply for SSI (if you think you are eligible).

Maximum Benefit Rate

The maximum benefit rate is the maximum monthly cash welfare benefit that can be awarded to individuals and couples. In California it is the Federal Benefit Rate (FBR) plus a State Supplement Payment (SSP).

Federal Benefit Rate

The Federal Benefit Rate (FBR) is based on the Consumer Price Index (CPI) and is revised annually. The rate takes effect on January 1st of each year. For 2003 the rates are:

- Individual FBR: $552
- Couple FBR: $829

California Maximum Benefit Rate

Some states also provide a supplement to the Federal assistance. California is one of these states. The amount of the state supplement is added to the FBR to determine the threshold for qualifying for SSI. Since June 2003, the SSP is $226 for individuals and $553 for a couple. So, for aged people living independently, the maximum benefit rates are:

- Individuals: FBR plus $226 = **$778.00**
- Couple: FBR plus $553 = **$1,382.00**

⮑ This is basically the eligibility level for Medi-Cal also.

🕸 Go to http://www.ssas.com/ca-ssi-2003-2.pdf for a full list of SSP rates for different conditions.

Income and Resource Rules for SSI

Elaborate rules govern how your income and resources are counted for SSI eligibility.

- **Income** determines eligibility as well as rate of payment.
- **Resources** determine eligibility, but *not* the rate of payment.

Certain kinds of income and resources are exempted and don't count towards your SSI eligibility.

What is the Difference Between Income and Resources

- Any lump sum payment received at any time during the month is considered as income for that month. *In-kind* income also counts.
- If not spent down, the income is considered to be a resource in *subsequent* months.

Non-Cash ("In Kind") Income and Resources

Not only cash counts towards income and resources. For example, if another person pays some of your rent, or offers you reduced rent, or pays for your food or clothing, this is considered *in-kind income* in the month it is received. Real estate, other than the house you live in, and insurance policies where you are the beneficiary, are also considered as your resources.

⟳ Assistance with food, clothing, or shelter expenditures is countable income by the SSA. If your family assists with other essentials, such as automobile expenses, your SSI may not be affected. See "In-Kind" Assistance Guidelines on page 48 for more details.

Fair Market Value Rules

Under provisions of the Personal Responsibility Act, you can lose benefits, for example, if you misreport real or personal properties. There are also rules regarding transfer of assets for less than market value, and if you do transfer assets for less than market value, rules determine a period of ineligibility for SSI on that account.

Income Limits

SSA subtracts your Countable Income from the Federal Benefit Rate (plus state supplement). The remainder is the amount of your cash benefit. Different rules apply if you are working. The exemptions are:

* Unearned income of up to $20 per month
* Earned and unearned income combined of up to $85 per month.

You can earn money and still receive benefits, as explained next.

Earned Income Limits – Work Incentives

Generally, if you are employed and have countable earnings over $800 (2003), you are considered to be engaging in Substantial Gainful Activity (SGA). You are not eligible for SSI in this case.

However, if you were already on SSI and then begin to earn money, you qualify for a Work Incentive program. This is to encourage people to return to work.

Go to http://www.ssa.gov/work/ResourcesToolkit/redbook.html for information about working while disabled.

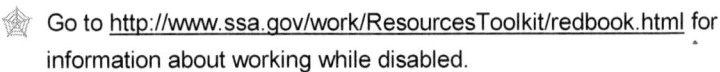

Work Incentives are now also known as **Employment Supports**.

Work Incentive Program 1619a – Earned Income

A Work Incentive program, known as 1619a, allows SSI recipients to earn income of **up to twice** the Federal Benefit Rate (FBR), plus state supplement, plus the earned and unearned income exemptions mentioned above, and still qualify for some benefit.

If you are an SSI recipient and go to work, then SSA does not count the first $65 per month of your countable earnings and half of the remainder when determining whether and how much your SSI cash benefit should be reduced.

This $65 plus half of the remainder is an "Earned Income Exclusion." This means that SSA counts less than half of your earnings when figuring your SSI cash benefit amount.

If you have no unearned income, then $20 per month is also excluded from your earned income before subtracting half of the remainder. If you do have unearned income, the $20 is subtracted from that amount to determine how much your cash benefit is reduced because of your unearned income. If your unearned income is less than $20, then the amount of your General Income Exclusion that is left over is subtracted from your earned income prior to subtracting half of the remainder.

The maximum SSI payments are (with the California State Supplement Payment)

- Individuals: $552 plus $226 = **$778.00**
- Couple: $829 plus $553 = **$1,382.00**

For example, for a married couple both eligible for SSI where one person works: take the maximum SSI payment, multiply by 2 (because half of it is exempt) and add $85 (which is also exempt). The result is $2849. The maximum the couple can earn and still be eligible for SSI must be $2845 or less.

To figure your benefit, deduct $ 85 from your earnings, and then divide the result by two. The result must be less than the maximum SSI payment – two dollars less for a couple, one dollar less for a single person.

> You may think a small SSI benefit is not worth applying for. But because you qualify for SSI, you qualify for Medi-Cal benefits too, as long as your resources meet the required limits. Also see next.

Work Incentive Program 1619b – Medicaid Eligibility

Even if the amount you earn is above the limit for the 1619a Work Incentive program, you may still be eligible for free Medi-Cal under the SSI Work Incentive program called 1619b.

The 1619b incentive provides continued Medicaid coverage for SSI recipients whose earnings are too high to allow an SSI cash payment.

To qualify for this incentive, you must meet the following requirements:

- You have been eligible for an SSI cash payment for at least one month
- You still meet other SSI eligibility requirements
- You need Medicaid in order to work
- You have gross earned income either below the state threshold level, which is $26,837.00 for California (2003), or below a higher individualized threshold, if you satisfy various other criteria, such as higher than average medical expenses.

Medicaid Need Test

When your earnings are such that you no longer qualify for an SSI cash benefit, you can retain Medicaid coverage if you need Medicaid in order to work. If you answer "Yes" to any of these questions, you need Medicaid (Medi-Cal) in order to work:

- Have you used any medical care or services in the past 12 months that was paid for by Medicaid?

- Do you expect to receive any medical care or services in the next 12 months that will be paid for by Medicaid?
- Without Medicaid, would you be unable to pay your medical bills if you become ill or injured in the next 12 months?

Go to http://policy.ssa.gov/poms.nsf/lnx/0502302040 to see the POMS reference: SI 02302.040.

Resource Limits

Go to http://www.vcu-barc.org/downloads/SSIResources.pdf for a thorough overview of 2003 SSI resources rules.

Resources are calculated on a month-to-month basis. Your resources are monies in your possession that you did not earn or otherwise acquire during that month.

Basically, the maximum limit on resources is $2000 for a single person, and $3000 for a couple, even if one of them is an ineligible spouse.

- Some resources are exempt and don't count towards SSI eligibility limits. This is explained in the next section.
- You can reduce your resources to meet the limits by *spending down* income in the month it is received. This is a legitimate way to avoid any adverse effect on SSI and Medi-Cal benefits. See "Spending Down Rules" on page 88 for details.

Effects of Repatriation of Rupees

It used to be that the Indian rupee was not fully convertible to U.S. dollars. Therefore Indians with resources in India could claim welfare benefits because their Indian resources were unavailable to them in the U.S. Because the Indian rupee is now becoming almost fully convertible to U.S. dollars, it is likely that some welfare claimants may become eligible to receive a considerable amount in U.S. dollars by way of Repatriation. If the amount is not large, you can spend down the money in the month you receive it so that it does not become part of the following month's resources.

Exempt and Non-Exempt Resources

Not all resources are counted for SSI eligibility. Exempt resources are not counted towards the resource limits, but non-exempt resources are.

Examples of Exempt Resources

- Home and home furnishings
- Car
- Computer
- Clothing

Examples of Non-Exempt Resources

- Cash
- Property other than the house you live in.
- Insurance policies that pay a large cash benefit to the claimant.

Reducing Non-Exempt Resources

The following are ways to reduce non-exempt property without incurring a period of ineligibility. See also Spending Down Rules, below.

- Pay medical bills

- Buy furnishings for the home
- Pay home mortgage
- Make repairs to the home
- Buy clothes
- Pay off other debts
- Pay off your auto loan
- Begin the process of liquidating non-liquid non-exempt assets. While such processes are occurring, the assets are not considered as resources because they are unavailable to you. For example, while a property is listed for sale, it is not considered to be your resource (see next section).
- Borrow against property to cover the cost of medical care, or request the medical provider to place a lien against the property to cover the cost of the care.

Real Estate That Cannot be Sold

Real property is excluded from an individual's or couple's resources for so long as it cannot be sold because:

- The property is jointly owned with another owner(s) whose principal place of residence the property is, and sale would cause undue hardship (due to loss of housing) to the other owner(s). (Funds held in a sole ownership account are presumed to be the property of the account holder in whose name the account is established, and such a presumption is not rebuttable even though the account holder does not consider him or herself to be the sole owner of the funds.)
- The owner's reasonable efforts to sell have been unsuccessful. (Reasonable but unsuccessful efforts to sell are evaluated initially under a 9-month conditional benefits arrangement; thereafter. the property is excluded outright for so long as it can not be sold.)

Spending Down Rules

If you have more resources than the prescribed limit for SSI, you can **spend down** those resources to below the limit, and reapply. Spending down refers to reducing resources by spending them on legitimate living expenses or on repayment of a loan.

There are rules governing what you can spend down on. In counting resources, a house, a car, computer, and other assets for daily requirements are exempted.

Insurance Policies

Insurance policies that have a large cash-in value to the holder of the policy are not exempt resources. However, insurance policies that benefit others, such as those intended to cover funeral expenses, are exempt.

Transfer of Assets

If you give away or sell a resource (assets) at *less* than fair market value on or after December 13, 1999, you may be ineligible for SSI for up to 30 months.

The Social Security Agency also has to report such a transfer to the state Medicaid Agency. A transfer of assets may result in a period of ineligibility for some Medicaid covered nursing home services.

Rules Concerning Loans

Because family members tend to help each other in times of difficulty, it is important to clearly understand the rules about giving and receiving loans

Definition of a Loan

A loan is an advance from lender to borrower that the borrower must repay, with or without interest. A loan can be cash or an in-kind advance in lieu of cash.

For example, an advance of food and shelter can represent a loan of the pro rata share of household operating expenses.

This applies to any commercial or non-commercial loan (between relatives, friends or others) that is recognized as enforceable under State law. The loan agreement may be oral or written, as long as it is enforceable under State law.

Money or an in-kind advance in lieu of cash given and accepted based on any understanding other than that it is to be repaid by the receiver is not considered to be a loan for SSI purposes.

For example, it could be a gift, support payments, in-kind support and maintenance etc., and must be treated as provided for in the rules applicable to such items.

Documentation of a Loan

Evidence must be obtained with respect to the existence of a bona fide loan agreement. The burden of proof with respect to the bona fide nature of the loan is with the applicant or recipient. However, loans between parents and children do not require documentary evidence.

A Loan is not Considered as Income

Any advance an SSI applicant or recipient receives that meets the above definition of a loan is not income for SSI purposes since it is subject to repayment.

A Loan is a Resource of Both Borrower and Lender

For borrowers: Any portion of the borrowed funds that the borrower does not spend in the month following receipt is considered to be the borrower's countable resource.

For Lenders: The loan agreement is considered a resource of the lender for SSI purposes, but the lender can rebut this presumption.

For example, an SSI recipient reports making a loan to a relative. The loan agreement is oral. The oral agreement is found to be binding under State law. Accordingly, the loan is presumed to be a resource of the lender because it can be converted to cash if the lender calls for repayment from the borrower. The lender can *rebut* this presumption by showing that the loan cannot be converted to cash – for example, because the borrower died without leaving an estate.

Money a lender receives as repayment of a loan reduces the outstanding loan balance and is considered a countable resource of the lender inasmuch as the repayment amount represents a return of part of the loan repayment. In other words, the total value of the resource (the repayment amount plus the outstanding loan balance) remains unchanged.

Interest on a loan is counted as unearned income to the lender in the month of receipt and if retained, is considered as a resource.

Rules Concerning Trust Funds

If you have a lump sum of money, you can form an irrevocable trust fund of real and/or personal property, where the beneficiary of the trust is one or more people other than yourself.

An irrevocable trust created to dispose of a large lump sum may fall under the provision of "Disposal of resources for less than Fair Market Value." Loss of benefits for a maximum three years period may be incurred, if this is the case. During this period, SSI will be discontinued.

If claimants face severe problems because of the loss of benefits, it is their responsibility to provide convincing proof for the hardships faced. It is possible that the Agency may resume the benefits.

Medicaid and Trust Fund Rules

If you are ineligible for SSI because of an irrevocable trust fund, you can probably still be eligible for Medi-Cal. The Medi-Cal Agency does not follow the same trust fund rules as the SSA. California uses SSI criteria to determine eligibility for Medi-Cal. But if an individual is *not* receiving SSI, the state may *not* use the SSI trust rules to determine eligibility for Medi-Cal. See "Trust Fund Rules – Different from SSI," on page 111.

Rules Concerning Living Arrangements

The amount of your SSI benefit is decided on the basis of your living arrangements. Typically, claimants are either living with family, or are renting, either from a family member or other person. The basic guideline is that you have to prove that you are paying your fair share of living expenses in order to receive full SSI benefits.

If you live in another's household and cannot or do not pay your way, you are considered to be receiving free board and lodging, even if you in fact pay part of the costs, and the cost of food and shelter is deducted from your SSI benefits. Your SSI payment is reduced, typically, by about a third.

Those Who Receive the Full Benefit

People in these categories receive full benefits:

* Those living alone as an individual or couple.
* Those who own their own home, or have rental payments.
* Those who live in a household where all members receive some form of public assistance
* Members of a household who purchase and consume food separately from other members of the household.
* Those who pay a *pro rata* share of the household expenses. (See below for more on this.)
* Those who pay a flat rate fee for both room and board.
* Those who rent a room in a house or apartment, and prepare meals separately.
* Those who live in someone else's household but do not receive free or subsidized food and shelter from anyone in the household.
* Those who live in an institution where Medicaid does not pay at least 50% of the costs.

Those Who Receive the Reduced Benefit

People who live in someone else's household and do not pay a pro rata share of household do not receive full benefits. Their benefits are reduced typically by a third. The pro rata share is explained next.

Paying a Pro Rata Share of Household Expenses

If you live in someone else's household, such as that of your son or daughter, the rules state that you are receiving free board and lodging unless you pay a *pro rata share* of household expenditures, also sometimes called a proportionate share.

To determine your pro rata share, the total household operating expenses are figured out or estimated. This figure is then divided by the number of people living in the home, including children. This is the pro rata share for each person.

For example, the pro rata share for a mother and father living with a son and his wife is half of the household expenditure. For a parent living with a daughter and her husband and their five children, the pro rata share for the parent is one eighth of household expenses.

To determine the pro rata amount (and that it is paid), the *head of household* completes a form showing how much he or she spends on each item of household expenditure, and how much the welfare claimant shares.

⮑ It is better to pay a little more than the pro rata share.

SSI Application Form

The SSA has introduced a new application form for SSI (**SSA-8000-BK**). Part II deals with Living Arrangements. The questions determine clearly if you qualify for full benefits or not.

For more information on the pro rata share, see
www.socialsecurity.gov/OP_Home/cfr20/416/416-1133.htm

Here is a quote from the above resource:

> Your pro rata share of household operating expenses is the average
> monthly household operating expenses (based on a reasonable
> estimate if exact figures are not available) divided by the number of
> people in the household, regardless of age.

What Are Household Expenses

The expenditures that are counted as household expenses include
the following.

* Mortgage, property tax and property insurance
* Rent
* Food
* Utilities: heating fuel, gas, electricity, water, garbage
  collection, sewer fees.

Phone expenses and household repairs are not classed as
household expenditure.

Business Arrangement: Renting

If you are renting living space (such as rooms, an apartment, or a
house) and preparing your own food, you can use the provision of
a business arrangement, instead of the pro rata share of cost.

A business arrangement exists when the amount of monthly rent
you pay is the same as the current Market Rental Value.

In situations where the landlord-tenant relationship is other than a
parent-child relationship the agency will presume that the amount

of monthly rent required to be paid equals the current market rental value. Where such relationship exists, the agency will try to find out whether the claimant gets "economic benefit" from the family relationship. The difference between market value and the rent paid is considered to be unearned income, also known as in-kind income, because the claimant is paying a subsidized rent.

The Court has held that if the proportion of income that the SSI recipient spends on housing according to these rules is "so great that it flies in the face of reality" then the difference is not considered as unearned income.

One-Third Reduction and Presumed Maximum Value Rules

One-Third Reduction (VTR) rule: If you live in another person's household and receive BOTH food and shelter, your grant will be reduced by one third.

> The applicable FBR is reduced by one-third when an individual/couple lives throughout a month in another person's household and receives **both** food and shelter from others living in the household. This reduction in the FBR has an income value, known as the value of the one-third reduction, or VTR.

(POMS manual, SI 00835.200, "The One-Third Reduction Provision — General" at http://policy.ssa.gov/poms.nsf/lnx/0500835200)

You lose one third, even if you pay a substantial amount of your share, but it falls short of the full pro rata share! The only way to rebut the one third reduction is to argue that the pro rata share is so large it *"flies in the face of reality"* to think that any difference between what you pay and the pro rata share is actually available to you as funds you can spend. In the San Francisco Bay Area, with its high housing costs, this is often possible.

Presumed Maximum Value (PMV) rule: If you live in your own household, or in another person's household and do NOT receive BOTH food and shelter, your grant will be reduced by the amount of the in-kind support and maintenance you receive (See "How the Presumed Value Rule Works" below for the procedure):

When an individual/couple receives in-kind support and maintenance (ISM), but does **not** receive **both** food and shelter from the household in which the individual/couple lives, the value of the one-third reduction (VTR) rule does not apply and the ISM is valued under the presumed maximum value (PMV) rule.

[Definition] The PMV is a regulatory cap on the amount of ISM that can be charged. Any food, clothing, or shelter received is presumed to be worth a maximum value.

[Rebuttal] The PMV is the **maximum** amount of ISM that may be charged. The PMV is not charged if an SSI claimant shows that:

• The current market value (CMV) of any food, clothing, or shelter received, minus any payment the claimant makes for them, is less than the PMV; or

• The actual amount someone else pays for the claimant's food, clothing, or shelter is less than the PMV.

(POMS manual, SI 00835.300, "Presumed Maximum Value Rule" at http://policy.ssa.gov/poms.nsf/lnx/0500835300)

How the Presumed Value Rule Works

If you are found to be receiving in-kind income related to food or shelter, the "presumed value" rule determines the maximum amount by which your SSI grant can be reduced for in-kind income for either food or shelter.

Initially, your SSI grant is reduced by one-third of the Federal benefit level plus $20. However, you are expected to rebut this with evidence that the actual value of support received was less than this.

So – suppose you live in your son's household and share family meals, and your payment to your son is $30 short of the full pro rata share – you lose one third of your grant. But suppose you eat your food separately, and pay your son a market rent for your room, and your son contributes $30 for your food budget, then you lose $30 of your SSI grant (that is, the "actual value" of the contribution).

It would be better in the above case for your son to contribute the $30 to your phone bill. This is not considered in-kind support and maintenance because it doesn't pay for food and shelter, and it cannot be converted to cash — so it does not impact your SSI benefit.

Domestic Service Rules

Domestic service by a parent for his or her son or daughter in or about the private home of the son or daughter is covered by Social Security beginning January 1, 1968 if any of the following is true:

- There is a genuine employment relationship between parent or son or daughter
- The son or daughter who employs the parent is living in his other private home a child who is under age 18, or if the child has a mental or physical condition that requires the personal care or supervision of an adult for at least four continuous weeks in the calendar quarter in which the domestic service is rendered; and
- The employer is a widow or widower; or his divorced and is not remarried; or has a spouse living in the home and the spouse has a physical or mental condition that renders him or her incapable of taking care of the child for at least four continuous weeks in a calendar quarter in which the parent performs the domestic service. The term child includes adopted child and a stepchild.

Change in Circumstances Rules

As a welfare recipient, you must report events or changes in circumstances if they affect your eligibility or payment amount.

You can report changes by phone or mail. To report by phone, call: 1–800–772–1213.

Go to http://www.ssa.gov/pubs/11011.html#part2 for complete details.

What Changes Must You Report?

Welfare recipients must report events that might affect eligibility for benefits, such as:

- Temporary absence from the U.S. or from the State of residence (see below)
- Change in amount of earned and unearned income and resources – for yourself, other beneficiaries, and any others whose income and resources are attributed to the welfare recipients
- Change of residence
- Marriage, divorce or separation
- Change in composition of the household
- Improvement in the condition that created a disability
- Eligibility for other benefits
- Change in school attendance
- Change in citizenship or alien status
- Becoming a fugitive felon, or violating a condition of probation or parole

When to Report Changes

You must report changes within 10 calendar days after the end of the month in which the event or change occurred.

If You Travel

However, if you travel outside the country for 30 days or more, or outside the state of residence for 60 days or more (see below), you must inform the SSA **before** you leave, giving dates of departure and arrival.

Absence from State of Residence for 60 or More Days

Rules may vary by state. When a person is absent from the state of California for more than 60 days, it shall be presumed to be a change of residence unless you inform the SSA in writing, both:

* An intent to return to California, and
* The existence of any of the following circumstances:
    * Illness or emergency which prohibit the return
    * Family members with whom the beneficiary lives are California residents and are physically present in the State
    * The beneficiary maintains California housing arrangements

Absence From U.S for 30 or More Days

If you leave the US for 30 days or more, you may become ineligible for SSI for that period, and for 30 days after your return.

Effect of Travel on SSI Benefits

If you leave the U.S. for more than thirty days, you are ineligible for SSI for the month of your absence, and for 30 days after you return.

If you are not eligible for SSI, you are also not eligible for Medi-Cal, if you qualify for it through SSI. Medi-Cal is automatically cancelled when SSI is cancelled.

Dates of Travel

The dates of your travel are also important. The government counts months from the first of the month. For example, if you leave the country on the second of April, and return on the third of May, you get benefits for April (because you were here on the first of the month), but no benefits for May, or for June.

Planning for Repatriation of Resources

If you have some resources abroad that you can now access (for example, you can now repatriate rupees from India), you can plan your travel to acquire your resources. You may use them for the travel expense and for living expenses for the month after your return, when you are not eligible for SSI benefits. You can also use this period to spend down your resources on necessities, so you are again eligible for SSI.

If Your SSI is Cancelled

Your SSI may be cancelled for various reasons. For example, if you give away property, you are not eligible for SSI for a three-year period. Until recently, you were also ineligible for Medi-Cal through SSI for such periods. However, this rule has changed. Your Medi-Cal should not be stopped until your case is considered. See "Craig V. Bonta: Keeping Medi-Cal When Benefits are Stopped" on page 53 for details about this change.

Medicare is NOT Automatically Cancelled

If you receive Medicare through the Medi-Cal program, and your Medi-Cal is cancelled, your Medicare is NOT automatically cancelled. You will be billed for Medicare premium payments if you do not phone or write to the SSA to cancel your Medicare benefit.

See "Immigrant Eligibility Requirements" on page 106 for a summary of the premium costs.

> ⟳ If you do not cancel Medicare, you will have to repay the Medicare for any period during which you were ineligible for welfare.

So, if you leave the country, phone or write to the SSA telling them that you wish to cancel SSI, Medi-Cal, *and Medi-Care* due to travel and provide the details.

Applying to Restore Medicare Coverage

When you come back, you must apply again for Medicare A during January, February, or March, and Medicare coverage begins in July. For Medicare B, you can at any time of the year.

Some Reasons for NOT Canceling Medicare

You may NOT want to stop Medicare. For example, you may be signed up with an HMO that provides coverage in the country you are traveling to, and you want to maintain medical insurance. Or, you may need surgery immediately on your return and don't want to wait for the Medi-Cal permission which takes maybe a week. In this case, be prepared to pay the Medicare premium for the period of ineligibility.

Some Legal Rights Regarding SSA Payments

Things change. You are not assured of future welfare or social security payments, and in general such payments cannot be garnished, except for child support and tax payments:

> Generally, Social Security benefits are exempt from execution, levy, attachment, garnishment, or other legal process, or from the operation of any bankruptcy or insolvency law. The exceptions are that benefits are subject: (1) to the authority of the Secretary of the Treasury to make levies for the collection of delinquent Federal taxes and under certain circumstances delinquent child support payments; and (2) to garnishment or similar legal process brought by an individual to enforce a child support or alimony obligation.

Quoted from: SSR 79-4: SECTIONS 207, 452(b), 459 and 462(f) (42 U.S.C. 407, 652(b), 659 and 662(f)) LEVY AND GARNISHMENT OF BENEFITS

Chapter 8
Medicare and Medi-Cal Rules

In the state of California, basic health care is available for all elderly people. If you have good income and resources, you are expected to use them to pay medical bills; if you have limited income and resources, you will qualify for state assistance under one of several programs, briefly described in this chapter.

This chapter is just a starting point. If you think you are eligible for a program, contact the SSA (for Medicare) or your county welfare office (for Medi-Cal) and make an application.

This chapter has sections on the following topics:

Resources

 Go to www.medicare.gov for more information on Medicare.

 Go to www.calmedicare.org for information provided by the California HealthCare Foundation (http://www.chcf.org) "an independent philanthropy committed to improving California's health care delivery and financing systems."

 Go to http://www.healthconsumer.org/Medi-CalOverview.pdf for a book-length resource on Medi-Cal published by the Health Consumer Alliance

To receive helpful booklets or talk to a Medicare representative, call 1-800-633-4227 24 hours a day for questions.

Medicare

Medicare is the U.S. health care program for seniors who have worked in the U.S. and are retired. It consists of three parts:

- Hospital Insurance (HI), known as Medicare Part A. The premium is $316.00.
- Supplementary Medical Insurance (SMI), known as Medicare Part B, which covers doctor visits and other outpatient services. The premium is $58.70.
- Medicare + Choice, known as Part C (established in 1997)

Parts A and B are also known as the Original Medicare Plan.

Whether you are responsible for paying the premiums or not depends on your eligibility. People who have Medicare A and B must meet the 20% coinsurance costs, and meet the annual deductibles before the benefit is paid. There are also limits on benefits provided, such as prescription benefits. Some healthcare, such as dental and optometry, is not included.

Part C, the Medicare + Choice program, (pronounced, "Medicare plus Choice") is an alternative to the Original Medicare Plan. The Medicare + Choice plan integrates Medicare with services provided by private healthcare providers such as Health Management Organizations (HMOs) to provide more benefits and (sometimes) less out-of-pocket expenses to recipients.

Another Medicare program that can be purchased is Medigap. This is a supplemental insurance provided by private insurance companies, to cover some of the services not covered by Medicare A and B.

Immigrant Eligibility Requirements

The following groups of immigrants are eligible for Medicare.

🔄 Citizenship is not a consideration for eligibility, but you must in all cases have completed 5 years of residency without a gap of 6 months or more outside the U.S.

- **Those over 65 with 40 credits or more.**
    - Medicare A is provided free and you pay the premium for Medicare B (The $58.70 premium is deducted from your monthly Social Security payment).
    - If your income and resources are low you may qualify for the QMB program, which pays for Part B.
- **Those over 65 with 30 – 40 credits**
    - You pay part of the monthly Medicare A premium, currently $174.00. You also pay the Medicare B monthly premium of $58.70.
- **Those over 65 with few or no credits who can afford to pay Medicare premiums**
    - As in all cases, you must have completed 5 years residency without a break of six months or more outside the U.S.

- You can buy B only, or A and B both. You cannot buy A only.
- If you don't buy coverage at age 65, but wait until you are older, the premium will cost more.
- **Those over 65 with few or no credits who have completed 5 years residency, and have limited income and resources**: If you are eligible for Medi-Cal, Medi-Cal will pay your Medicare costs. If your income is a little higher, you may qualify for a Medi-Cal program that covers some of your Medicare costs. This is explained in the following section.

Medi-Cal

Almost all seniors with modest resources can qualify for a Medi-Cal program. In general, Medi-Cal covers all medical expenses (unlike Medicare). Details are provided in Medi-Cal booklets you can send for, as well as on the web sites shown below.

What is Medi-Cal?

Medi-Cal is the name given to Medicaid in California. Medicaid is a Federal program to provide healthcare to two main groups: the medically needy and the medically indigent. Many elderly people are included in the medically needy category, even if they have reasonably good income. Those who are somewhat better off may be eligible if they pay a share of cost. For a general overview of Medicaid, see page 70.

Some counties have supplementary programs too. Check with your county of residence.

Medi-Cal Resources

 Go to http://cms.hhs.gov/medicaid for Federal Medicaid information.

 Go to www.medi-cal.ca.gov for Information about Medi-Cal.

 Go to http://www.medi-cal.org for information provided by the California HealthCare Foundation (http://www.chcf.org) "an independent philanthropy committed to improving California's health care delivery and financing systems."

To get help in choosing the best healthcare options available to you, you can call Health Insurance Counseling and Advocacy Program (HICAP) at 1-800-434-0222.

To receive helpful booklets or talk to a Medi-Cal officer, call your local county welfare office, which is in the Government pages of your phone book.

Applying for Medi-Cal Related Benefits

Apply to your county welfare department, which you can find in the Government pages in the phone book. It could be that the county will give you Medi-Cal even if your resources are over the Medi-Cal limit.

If you are a "dual eligible" – that is, eligible for Medi-Cal and Medicare, you can call the SSA hotline at 1-800-772-1213 to make an appointment with your local field office.

You can request an interpreter be present. In some states, the SSA representative can complete the application. In other states, you must take the completed SSA paperwork to your welfare office and complete additional paperwork.

When Does Medi-Cal Coverage Begin?

Medi-Cal coverage may begin as early as the third month prior to application, if you would have been eligible for Medicaid, had you applied during that time. If you had medical expenses during that period, they should be covered.

Out of State Authorization for Treatment

If you need immediate treatment while you are out of state, Medi-Cal will generally pay. In order for out-of-state providers to bill Medi-Cal, they must first obtain a provider number, an out-of-state manual, and the appropriate forms from:

Department of Health Services
San Francisco Medi-Cal Field Office
P.O. Box 3704
San Francisco, CA 94119
(415) 904- 9600

Medi-Cal and Medicare Compared

Medicare is the health plan for most retired people who are fully insured. Retired people who are not fully insured and who have limited income and resources can get Medi-Cal instead. Because it is intended to benefit people with very little income and resources, Medi-Cal covers more expenses than Medicare, for example, dental, hearing, and optometry, if you can find a health provider who will accept Medi-Cal. You may find that fewer doctors will take Medi-Cal as payment, because the payment is low.

Medicare recipients have to pay co-insurance, deductibles, and premiums. However some new options get around this limitation to some extent.

➲ Medi-Cal itself often pays for Medicare expenses.

Medicare With No-Cost Medi-Cal

If you are eligible for no-cost Medi-Cal coverage, the Medi-Cal program also pays for Medicare coverage. (They do this because it shifts the burden of cost for some services to the Federal, instead of the State budget.) Services that are covered by both programs will be paid first by Medicare and the difference is paid by Medi-Cal, up to the State's payment limit. Medi-Cal also covers additional services not covered by Medicare, for example, nursing facility care beyond Medicare's 100-day limit, prescription drugs, eyeglasses, and hearing aids.

Medi-Cal Eligibility

Immigrant Eligibility Rules

To be eligible for Medi-Cal, you must be a citizen or have a green card (be a permanent resident). PRUCOL aliens are also eligible to receive limited benefits such as emergency care. For example, those who have applied for permanent resident status are PRUCOL aliens.

↷ Apply for Medi-Cal as soon as your application for adjustment of status is accepted for consideration.

Immigration Status

Persons without Satisfactory Immigration Status may be eligible for Medi-Cal benefits restricted to emergency care and pregnancy services, if all other program requirements are met.

If you are an alien applying for or receiving Restricted Medi-Cal benefits only, you are not required to give the county welfare Department information about the immigration status, place or birth, or social security number of yourself or any member of your family requesting or receiving restricted benefits.

(Extract from MC information Notice 009(4/91))

Categorically Eligible Groups

States that receive Federal funding must provide medical coverage for certain individuals who receive Federal assistance. Generally, Federal funds are provided for *categorically needy* groups. Children, pregnant women, recipients of foster care assistance, and other *categorical groups* in need have to be medically covered by Federal benefits.

Trust Fund Rules – Different from SSI

The Medicaid Act is amended for states that provide noncategorical Medicaid and use SSI criteria to determine eligibility. If the individual is not "receiving" SSI, the State may not use the SSI trust rules to determine eligibility for noncategorical Medicaid. Irrevocable trust funds do not count as your resources for Medi-Cal eligibility (see the POMS 89.7). Other rules apply to individuals who qualify for Medi-Cal because they fall into a category that is always covered.

Income and Resource Eligibility Rules

You may qualify for free Medi-Cal if you meet SSI income and resource eligibility rules (with the exception that your resources can be twice the SSI resource limits). You can qualify for other programs if your resources are within limits but your income is over limits, for example, Medi-Cal with share of cost. The rules are complex. A basic explanation is given in the following sections about eligibility rules. Because eligibility conditions are different for the various programs, it is difficult to summarize in a table.

If your **resources are within limits** but your **income is over the limits**, apply to the county welfare agency if you think you might be eligible for one of the many Medi-Cal programs. There are many rules, and the welfare officer will help determine your eligibility.

No-Cost Medi-Cal Eligibility Rules

The following groups of people are eligible for no-cost Medi-Cal.

Those Who Receive SSI

If you receive SSI, you automatically receive no-cost Medi-Cal.

↪ If your SSI is cancelled, your Medi-Cal is also automatically cancelled. If this happens to you, immediately apply to the county welfare office to reinstate Medi-Cal. See the section, "If Your SSI is Cancelled" on page 101.

Those Who Are Eligible for SSI Except for Immigrant Status

Many people who don't qualify for SSI because of immigration status still qualify for free Medi-Cal. For example, you are eligible for Medi-Cal (but not SSI) during the sponsorship deeming period. In general, the income and resource rules used to determine Medi-Cal eligibility are the same as those used to determine SSI eligibility. One difference is that **Medi-Cal allows you to keep twice the resources as the SSI rules**.

Rules are a little different for property that is worth (to you) $2000 or less if you are single, $3000 or less if you are married. There are also various complex rules determining your case if things are not straightforward, for example, if your benefits are suspended or terminated for some other reason and then are resumed.

Medi-Cal Programs with Higher Eligibility Limits

If your income and resources are a little above Medi-Cal income and resources limits, you may still qualify for a program that helps with Medi-Cal or Medicare payments (if you are otherwise eligible for Medicare).

A&D FPL Program

The Aged and Disabled Federal Poverty Level (A&D FPL) program allows individuals with incomes up to 133% of the Federal Benefits Rate to receive free Medi-Cal and in home supportive services (IHSS). It is sometimes referred to as the Medi-Cal 133% program.

Share of Cost Medi-Cal

If your resources are within the Medi-Cal limit, but your income is above the limit, you may apply for Share of Cost Medi-Cal (also known as Medi-Cal with Share of Cost). With this program, you are responsible for all medical expenses up to a predetermined amount per month. Medi-Cal pays for allowable medical expenses over this amount.

In order for Medi-Cal to cover your medical expenses after you meet your share of cost, you must use providers that accept Medi-Cal.

Your share of cost is your net income minus the Medi-Cal "Maintenance Needs Level," which is $600 for a single person and $934 for a couple.

Your net income is determined by subtracting all the allowable deductions. There are about 40 allowable deductions, including deductions for educational expenses, dependent care, alimony payments, and an earned income deduction.

If medical bills leave you with less monthly income than the Medi-Cal "Maintenance Needs Level" (after allowable deductions) you may qualify for this program.

If your income is very high, the share of cost is also very high. However, the share of cost is only incurred when you incur medical expense, and it is a maximum limit. If your share of cost is determined to be $4000 per month, this is the maximum you would ever pay in a month. If your medical costs are $1,50 in a month, you pay $1,50 for that month.

Example: A single 70-year-old man is ineligible for SSI because his monthly Social Security income is $1,200. His "net" (countable) income is $1,180 ($1,200 less the standard $20 deduction). His "share of cost" will be $580 a month (his $1,180 net minus the State's $600 MNL). He has a medical bill of $1000. He is responsible for his $580 monthly "share-of-cost." Medi-Cal will pay the remaining $420. (Each year, the DPSS will determine his eligibility for the program and his monthly "share-of-cost.")

(Example quoted from: www.healthcarerights.org/medicare/medi-Cal)

Medi-Cal Buy-In Program for Working Disabled

California offers a Medi-Cal Buy-In program that allows individuals with disabilities who would not otherwise be eligible for Medi-Cal to gain Medi-Cal coverage. Those with resources within limits and with incomes over a specified amount are able to "buy-in" by paying a premium and deductible.

Dual-Eligibility Programs

Dual eligibles are individuals who are entitled to Medicare Part A and/or Part B and are eligible for some form of Medicaid benefit.

You must be eligible for Medicare to qualify for these programs, and also meet the other eligibility requirements, which are higher than for no-cost Medi-Cal. The **income limits** are compared against your actual income **minus exclusions**. Even if your income is a little higher than the limits, you may find that you qualify after exclusions.

> You can only sign up for Medicare A between January 1 and March 31. You can sign up for Medicare B at any time.

The following sections describing the various programs are based on this source: http://www.cms.gov/dualeligibles/bbadedef.asp

Specific income figures for each program can be found at: http://www.cms.gov/dualeligibles/4732rate.asp.

Federal Poverty Level

Some dual-eligibility criteria are based on the Federal Poverty Level (FPL). In 2003, the Federal Poverty Level is:

* $8,980 for a single person annually
* $11,210 for a couple annually

Qualified Medicare Beneficiaries (QMBs) without other Medicaid (QMB Only)

These individuals are entitled to Medicare Part A, have income of 100% Federal poverty level (FPL) or less and resources that do not exceed twice the limit for SSI eligibility, and are not otherwise eligible for full Medicaid.

Medicaid pays their Medicare Part A premiums, if any, Medicare Part B premiums, and, to the extent consistent with the Medicaid State plan, Medicare deductibles and coinsurance for Medicare services provided by Medicare providers.

QMBs with full Medicaid (QMB Plus)

These individuals are entitled to Medicare Part A, have income of 100% FPL or less and resources that do not exceed twice the limit for SSI eligibility, and are eligible for full Medicaid benefits. Medicaid pays their Medicare Part A premiums, if any, Medicare Part B premiums, and, to the extent consistent with the Medicaid State plan, Medicare deductibles and coinsurance, and provides full Medicaid benefits.

Specified Low-Income Medicare Beneficiaries (SLMBs) without other Medicaid (SLMB Only)

These individuals are entitled to Medicare Part A, have income of greater than 100% FPL, but less than 120% FPL and resources that do not exceed twice the limit for SSI eligibility, and are not otherwise eligible for Medicaid. Medicaid pays their Medicare Part B premiums only.

SLMBs with full Medicaid (SLMB Plus)

These individuals are entitled to Medicare Part A, have income of greater than 100% FPL, but less than 120% FPL and resources that do not in exceed twice the limit for SSI eligibility, and *are* eligible for full Medicaid benefits. Medicaid pays their Medicare Part B premiums and provides full Medicaid benefits.

Qualified Disabled and Working Individuals (QDWIs)

These individuals lost their Medicare Part A benefits due to their return to work. They are eligible to purchase Medicare Part A benefits, have income of 200% FPL or less and resources that do not exceed twice the limit for SSI eligibility, and are *not* otherwise eligible for Medicaid. Medicaid pays the Medicare Part A premiums only.

Other Medi-Cal Programs

Medi-Cal is not a single program. It is an overlapping patchwork of programs, some more of which are listed below.

* In-Home Support Service. Recipients of In-Home Support Service (IHSS) also receive Medi-Cal as a benefit of the program.
* Long Term Care Medi-Cal. Medi-Cal will cover Long Term Care (LTC) services if the individual is otherwise eligible for Medi-Cal. Special income and resources rules apply to a person in LTC who has a spouse at home.
* Hospice Care. Coverage for up to 210 days to terminally ill beneficiaries (those beneficiaries that have a medical prognosis of a six month or less expectancy). A person can be recertified and so receive hospice care for longer than 210 days.
* Persons Infected with Tuberculosis. This program has higher thresholds than no-cost Medi-Cal.
* Special Treatment Programs. This covers dialysis and hyperalimentation treatment. Income and resources rules differ from other Medi-Cal programs.
* No-Cost Health Coverage for Children Birth Through Age 18, and Pregnant Women. This program has higher thresholds. You can apply by mail without visiting the welfare office.
* Healthy Families – Low-Cost Health Coverage for Children Birth Through Age 18. Again, this program has higher thresholds than no-cost Medi-Cal.

Chapter 9
Frequently Asked Questions

How to Use This Chapter

This chapter contains many questions that are a digest of common situations I have encountered in my social work, helping people in need get the benefits for which they are eligible. The situations are real enough, though I have changed specifics and combined different similar cases to provide useful information.

Please read through this chapter looking for questions similar to your own. I hope the answers I provide help to resolve your uncertainties and provide a secure way forward.

Q 1 **I am a naturalized American citizen. I want to sponsor my parents. Is it necessary for them to come as a visitor or can I sponsor them when they are in India? What is more advantageous?**

Ans. It depends on the readiness of your parents to leave India. It may be less expensive to sponsor them from India. If they are in a city where there is no immigration office it might be better for them to come here first as visitors; otherwise they may be sponsored from India.

Q 2 **My daughter has sponsored my wife and me for the Green Card; I have heard that I will have to get Medical Insurance. I approached an insurance company but due to my ill health they are not willing to insure me. I am told that it will take a year before I get a Green Card and if I try to get welfare benefits from the welfare department, my Green Card will be in danger. What should I do?**

Ans. According to the present rules, if you have not exceeded your visa time, and if your application for a Green Card is approved, this will not hurt your chances of getting a Green Card. Medical benefits are not considered a public charge. (Other benefits such as cash benefits are considered a public charge.) But the rules are changing fast, so please check with your local county Social Services agency.

Q 3 My wife and I receive SSI and Medi-Cal. Recently my uncle died and he has left all his property to the other nephews. I am told that the will is defective and if I challenge I may win. Suppose I get about $10,000 from my uncle's property. Will it have any effect on my welfare benefits?

Ans. The month you receive the $10,000 your wife and you will lose SSI for that month. If you spend down $10,000 and bring your resources below $3000, your SSI will resume. So long as your legacy is treated as your unearned income, it will not be your resource. If you do not spend it down, you may lose both SSI and Medi-Cal till you bring your resources below $3000.

Q 4 I intend to leave the U.S. late in December and want to return before the end of January. As I am present for both the calendar months, I feel that my SSI, medical benefits will not be discontinued. Do I understand the rules correctly?

Ans. No, if you are absent from this country for 30 days continuously your SSI will be discontinued irrespective of your presence for both the calendar months till you come back and stay in this country for 30 days. The day of departure and the day of arrival are excluded from the calculation of absence.

Q 5   I stay with my daughter and get both SSI and Medi-Cal. My daughter is leaving the country for a short period. As my son lives in Virginia, I wish to go for 3-4 months to my son. As no passport entries are required for traveling within USA, is it necessary to inform the Social Security Agency? If I inform them, they may discontinue my SSI. What should I do?

Ans.   SSI is a Federal program and you do not lose it if you travel within the U.S. However, you must inform the Agency whenever you change your address even temporarily. You might lose your state supplement, however. Find out whether the state of Virginia gives Medicaid to non-citizens. Some states have no provisions for non-citizens. Explain to the Agency that your temporary absence is beyond your control, and that there is no change of residency. They will advise you correctly and it is possible that you will retain your state supplement. Please do not make the mistake of not informing the Agency; later on this may land you in trouble.

Q 6   I am going out of California for only 20 days. Do I need to inform the Social Security Agency?

Ans.   Yes. Those who are on welfare have to follow the rules to retain their benefits.

Q 7   My daughter sponsored my wife and me in January 1996. I have completed 65 years this month. I stay with my son,

who has an apartment. Do I qualify for any benefits such as Medi-Cal and cash?

Ans. If you got your Green Card before 22nd August 1996, your daughter is no longer under a legal obligation to maintain you, as the 5-year sponsorship period is over. You may qualify for CAPI benefits. However, to qualify for full CAPI benefits, you have to pay a pro rata share of the total expenditure of the family. If not, you are deemed to be getting free board and lodging and your benefits will be reduced to that extent. After 1996, the deeming period for CAPI was extended from 5 years to 10 years. It is worth applying, because you arrived before this change. If you don't get CAPI, you are still likely to get general assistance and food stamps if you are found otherwise eligible.

Q 8 **This year, which is the year 2002, my wife and I arrived in this country on permanent residence. While coming here I had brought $8000. The Medi-Cal department of welfare has refused to give me medical benefits on the ground that my assets are over the prescribed limit. They have stated in their denial letter that I have the right of appeal. What are the chances of my getting the medical benefits on appeal?**

Ans. On the month of you arrival, your $8000 is your income. If you do not spend it down, in the following month it would be your resource. Spend down the amount, and again apply for medical benefits. If you do so, there is no reason why medical benefits would be denied to your wife and you, if you were otherwise eligible.

Q 9 **I was receiving SSI because of disability. Recently they reviewed my case and declared that I am no longer**

disabled. What should I do to get my welfare benefits continued? I will be 65 within 3 months.

Ans. You have a right of appeal and during the process of appeal your benefits cannot be discontinued till you get a negative decision on your appeal. It is best to apply for an appeal within ten days of the review. If you apply before 10 days, your benefits will continue. If your appeal fails, you will have to repay the SSI (but not Medi-Cal). If you  apply after 10 days, SSI and Medi-Cal will be stopped, but if your appeal is successful, you will get the SSI benefit retroactively. Also – if you apply within 10 days, your appeal will probably be heard earlier.

Q 10 I arrived in this country in 2002. My daughter opened a joint account with me and deposited $2000 as a loan, so that I don't have to always be asking her for small loans. The Medi-Cal agency has considered all this $2000 as my resource and has denied medical benefits. I have the right of appeal. What are the chances for success if I go for appeal?

Ans. The rules say that a loan taken is not a resource. You need not go for an appeal. Ask for a review, and explain the rules to the caseworker. You have full chances of success. In any case, $2000 is within the prescribed limit, although free board and lodging from your daughter would be considered as your income.

Q 11   My SSI was discontinued for 2-3 months. On appeal I
have won the case and the appellate judge directed the
Agency to give me all back payments. I am likely to get
arrears for both my wife and me, amounting to about
$5000. But how can I keep my balance less than $3000,
when besides the amount of $ 5000 I shall continue to get
my monthly allowances?

Ans.   You will be informed by the Agency that you may keep
the balance above $3000 for at least 3 months. You have
ample time to spend the amount. Please consult the
Agency.

Q 12   My brother and I are joint owners of a house in India.
My brother doesn't want to sell it and he is not in a
position to buy my share. I fear that I will lose my SSI
and Medi-Cal benefits. Is there any way out?

Ans.   First of all, your brother must agree to sell the property or
to buy your share. If he does not agree to either of these
proposals you have a fair chance of getting the property
excluded. But remember that it must be a genuine denial
on his part and you must be able to convince the Agency.
In addition, because (in the first half of 2003) there are
currency restrictions making it impossible to get the
proceeds of the sale from rupees into dollars, the property
may be excluded.

Q 13   I am over 65 years of age and as my income is above
$2,500 per month I am refused Medi-Cal. If I buy
Medicare, what would be my monthly premium? Can I
get Medicare without getting Medi-Cal?

Ans.   If your income is such that you qualify for SSI, then you
will qualify for full Medi-Cal. Your income is too high to

qualify for SSI. However, your income is still quite low, so may still get Medi-Cal benefits if you pay some of the cost, as determined by the government. This is called "share of cost." Those who do not qualify for any Medi-Cal may think of buying Medicare. The total cost of Medicare A & B would be around $400 per month for you, and an additional $400 for your spouse, if you are married.

Q 14 **My daughter sponsored me in 1999. She had signed a legal affidavit, taking responsibility for me for five years. Both she and her husband are out of a job. They have got a house and a car but no other assets. Am I entitled to any benefits even before the completion of five years?**

Ans. While considering your SSI benefits her resources would be deemed to be your resources, please consult the Agency you have a fair chance of receiving CAPI if you are 65 years and above.

Q 15 **I am a disabled individual. I cannot afford to maintain my self and my family on the SSI given to me. I want to start a small business and want to borrow from friends and relatives the capital required to start the business.**

Some of the friends are prepared to give me the amount with a check, and others are willing to give in cash. Will starting a business and getting income from my business affect my SSI benefits?

Ans. I do not think that borrowing in cash would create any trouble for you with the Welfare department. The Agency encourages disabled people to work, and unless you earn too much from business, your benefits are not likely to be stopped. According to the current rules, the first $85 is exempted, and thereafter half of your earnings are also exempted. Even if you get SSI of just $1 your Medi-Cal benefits will not be stopped. Please work in consultation with the Agency.

Q 16 I am told that even though I am disabled, I can work. Earlier I worked in a company as an Assistant Accountant, but my wages were not large enough to disqualify me from SSI and Medi-Cal benefits. The manager is leaving for his country for a year. He has offered me his job and is prepared to pay me $4000 gross. I am likely to lose my SSI benefits. Is there any way to continue my Medi-Cal benefits for the full year?

Ans. Income is no bar to the continuance of Medi-Cal benefits, as long as your resources stay within the limit. However, you will have to pay a share of the cost. The Welfare Agency encourages disabled people to work. Consult the Agency for best advice.

Q 17 I am in receipt of welfare benefits including Medicare and SSI. If I go out of the country for 8 months will it affect my Medi-Cal and Medicare benefits?

Ans. Your Medi-Cal benefits will be automatically suspended when you report that you are leaving. However, Medicare is not suspended automatically. You must apply for discontinuance of the Medicare premium as soon as possible. If you don't, then you will have a Medicare premium bill to pay when you return, even if you don't normally pay the premium. When you come back, if you don't return during the three months application period, apply as a Qualified Medical Beneficiary (Q.M.B.) for Medicare A/B. This covers you until you can get the Medicare benefits reinstated. If you are a citizen, your Medi-Cal will be resumed upon your return. If you are not a citizen, your Medi-Cal is discontinued after a 6 months absence from the country. You should remember to apply for a 2-year re-entry permit before leaving to avoid BCIS difficulties.

Q 18 My son is less than 18 years old. He is disabled and is getting Medi-Cal benefits on the grounds of his disability. Can I get any allowances for him?

Ans. He can get allowances only if your income and resources deemed to be his are below the prescribed limit. However, you should apply, because there are certain exceptions for deeming for a disabled child under 18.

Q 19 I was out of this country for a period of five months. I sent a letter to the Agency, saying that my Medicare and SSI should be discontinued for this period. When I came back I found that, through a mistake, they had credited the entire five months amount to my account. Can I retain this amount, as there is no fault of mine?

Ans. "No fault" is one of the reasons for waiver of over-payment, but that is not enough. If you have genuine hardship in paying your bills you may apply for waiver. Otherwise you have to pay back the Agency. You may get easy installments.

Q 20 I stay with my son and other members of his family. We used to live in an apartment. I paid a pro rata share of the household expenditure. My son has now moved to a house and he has a large mortgage to pay. Will I have to increase my contribution to the household expenses, so that it still qualifies as a pro rata share? How will my share be counted?

Ans. If your son is prepared to rent a small part of the house to you, and if you prepare your own food, you will continue to get full SSI benefits. You must pay rent and buy your food. The rent should be a fair market rate. Make sure to consult the Agency to determine what is an acceptable rate. If you play fair with the Agency they are likely to help you.

Q 21   I am over 65 and also disabled. Because I am over 65, I am getting Medi-Cal benefits. I applied for getting my disability certified, but the Agency refused to consider this, because I am getting Medi-Cal benefits. Is there any advantage to appealing this decision getting my Medi-Cal benefits on grounds of disability?

Ans.   As disabled individuals also have a chance of getting in-home services, I feel you should appeal against the decision. Normally the Administrative Law Judge may not give the decision in your favor but it is worth appealing.

Q 22   I have resources of about $5000 and I meet all other qualifications for getting Medi-Cal and CAPI. The department desires that I should apply only after my resources are less than $3000. I am a married individual. What are the ways in which I can legally spend down my resources?

Ans.   If you have any debt for which you can give convincing proof, repay the debt. You may also spend down on personal needs like dress, food, travel, buying books etc. Please keep receipts for whatever you spend. You should have no difficulty spending down $2000 in order to qualify. Note that even if your wife is ineligible for SSI because of age, the limit is still $3000.

Q 23   I arrived in the U.S. in December 1997. I am completing five years on 13th December 2002. Am I entitled to CAPI benefits? I am already getting Medi-Cal benefits.

Ans.   In 2000, the CAPI deeming limits were extended from 5 years to 10 years, so you will not get CAPI. You may, however, apply for general assistance and food stamps.

Q 24 I am staying with my daughter. I desire to go to India for a period less than 30 days. My daughter has agreed to buy a return ticket for both of us. Will it have any effect on my welfare allowances?

Ans. Yes, if the ticket is a gift from your daughter, the cost of the ticket will be treated as your income and your SSI will be discontinued even though your absence is less than 30 days. However if she agrees to lend you the amount, and you may pay back in easy installments, your SSI will not be affected.

Q 25 I will reach the age of 65 years in May 2003, I am a citizen, and I am eligible for SSI, Medi-Cal and Medicare. What are the procedures to get all the three benefits?

Ans. You request an appointment with the Agency Manager and tell him or her that you intend to apply for all three benefits. You must keep all your documents ready, like passport, bank statements and any other proof of age and resources. It is better that you complete all the formalities by late April, so you get the benefit on your birthday in May.

Q 26 I get a monthly pension of $600 from the British government (after converting British currency to dollars). I have recently obtained American citizenship and I have no resources except the pension. Am I eligible for SSI, Medi-Cal and Medicare benefits?

Ans. Yes. If you are 65 years of age or disabled if younger, please contact the Agency manager for an appointment. He or she will advise you correctly.

Q 27   I stay with my elder son. He sponsored me 5 years ago. He pays my medical insurance and bears all my expenditure. I have no income. Am I eligible for any welfare benefits?

Ans.   Because you arrived after 1996, you are not eligible for CAPI or SSI. If you are 65 years or older, and have resources less than $4000, you may get Medi-Cal and save the expenditure of your son. (The limit is $4000 because you are not applying for SSI.) You may also apply for general assistance and food stamps, which is sort of a loan payable from future welfare cash benefits.

Q 28   I am to reach the age of 65 in September 2003. My son sponsored me and I arrived in the U.S. in September 1998. Will I be eligible for any welfare benefits in September 2003 and onwards? I am not a citizen.

Ans.   As you arrived after 22nd August 1996, you are not eligible for SSI. For the cash assistance program for immigrants known as CAPI, the sponsor's liability is extended from 5 years to 10 years. You are therefore eligible for Medi-Cal, and also Medicare if there is no break in residency for more than 6 months. You may apply for general assistance. Your resources must be within the prescribed limit.

Q 29   I have already completed the 40 quarters (10 years work) required for getting Social Security, and I am 61 years of age. Is it advisable for me to draw Social Security early, and still continue my job?

Ans.   You can draw Social Security at reduced rates once you are 62 years old. If you are confident that you will be able to continue in your job for many more years, you might want to do this. Otherwise it is advisable for you to wait till you are 66 years of age (and get the full amount), because you will get the reduced rate for the rest of your life. Please consult Social Security authorities.

Q 30 I came to this country only last year (2001). My wife accompanied me. Both of us have Green Cards. My

daughter-in-law is speaking a language that I do not understand. She curses me, abuses my wife and me and it is not possible to stay with self-respect. Can we get any benefits enabling us to stay separately?

Ans. Yes, if you can prove it to the satisfaction of the Agency.

Q 31 I have $8000 in my bank, but no other resource. I am told that if I spend the full amount, I can get welfare benefits on the basis of age—I am over 65. If I withdraw the amount and give it to my son, will the Social Security Agency question my action and deny me benefits?

Ans. Yes, unless you can prove that it was a repayment of a loan. You must spend down and bring the resources below $2000 if you are single, or below $3000 if you are married and are staying with your spouse.

Q 32 My son, who sponsored me 3 years back, is abusive. I want to stay with my brother but my brother expects me to pay $350 per month for board and lodging. Can I get any help from welfare?

Ans. Yes. You have to give convincing proof of your son's abusive treatment. As regards paying $350 to your brother, if it is a proportionate expenditure payment, and if you qualify on the basis of age, disabilities and income/resources, you will get welfare benefits. Even if the share is not proportionate, you will still get CAPI. See "Paying a Pro Rata Share of Household Expenses" on page 93 for more about the topic of a pro rata share.

Q 33 I stay with my son and son's wife. They have 3 children all below 18 years of age. My wife and I stay in a separate room and my wife cooks for herself and me. The welfare department does not pay us full SSI because they consider that we get free boarding and lodging. Is there any way by which I can get full SSI for my wife and myself?

Ans. You have to pay a pro rata share, which in your case would be two-sevenths (2/7) of the total share of expenditure, from mortgage to garbage. In addition, your son must include this amount as income on his tax return. If you cannot pay 2/7th of expenditure of the family, you have to pay him a fair-market rent for the room. Again, he must declare this as income on his tax return. You better consult the Agency and if your difficulty is genuine it will help you to get full share of SSI.

Q 34 I am on CAPI; I am told that those who are on CAPI can get food stamps. How much I would get, if I am otherwise eligible?

Ans. You will get the difference between SSI and CAPI payments, which is currently $10 a month for an individual, $20 for a couple.

Q 35 My wife and I stay with my daughter. My daughter's two sons are now over 18 years, and they stay in a university dormitory. My daughter is a divorcee. I cannot pay my proportional share of her expenditure, which comes to two-thirds. Is there any way in which we can get full SSI benefits?

Ans. Yes, if you can pay a fair-market rent and prepare your own food. Your daughter must also declare this as income on her tax return. Please consult the Agency; if your difficulty is genuine you may get its help.

Q 36 My wife and I come from Canada and have no legal status here. We do not get any welfare benefits. We cannot go to India because we will not be allowed to return and there is no one to take care of us. My son maintains us but is not willing to apply for adjustment of status. What is the way out, to get welfare at least medical?

Ans. Apply to the county welfare office and request them to write to BCIS to see if BCIS desires to deport either or both you. It is likely that BCIS will not so desire, as you are old and harmless. You can then get welfare benefits, both medical and cash.

Q 37   I stay with my son who sponsored me. He recently lost his job. He has a house, a car and plenty of resources. But if I stay long with him, his savings will soon be depleted. Can I get welfare benefits till he gets a job?

Ans.   The house and car are exempted resources. The other resources are considered to be your resources until the sponsorship period of five years is over. Because your son is out of work, there may be a way out. Please consult the SSI and CAPI agency.

Q 38   I am 95 years of age. Recently I lost my wife who used to take care of me. I suffer from sleeplessness and prostate problems. I am on SSI but I don't get hired help. My son and son's wife both work and maintain themselves with difficulty. Is there any way by which I can get help from welfare?

Ans.   Yes you can get in-home service. The welfare agency will send someone for limited hours to take care of you.

Q 39   I am 65 years of age. Because of my resources I am not eligible for welfare. Can I buy Medicare?

Ans.   You may buy Medicare if you are a citizen or you have completed 5 years of stay without a break of more than 6 months.

Q 40 I am getting SSI, Medi-Cal, and Medicare. I went out of the USA for four months. Though my medical card is operative I get bills for Medicare premium for A/B. I wrote to my SSI office but there is no reply from them, what should I do?

Ans. You may call 1-800-633-4227 and register your complaint. As you are on SSI the bills are not payable by you.

Q 41 I have both income and property in India. I am a Green Card holder and on welfare. I do not want to bring my funds over here; I have very old parents in India. They make use of them. How can I be compelled to bring my property and lose my welfare? Can the Welfare department compel me to apply for repatriation of my property?

Ans. Yes, if you want to retain your welfare benefits. Welfare is a program of last resort. You have to exhaust all your efforts to get your dues before you apply for welfare benefits. However, you do not have to sell the house if your parents live in it, and you may even make some provision for them if they have no other income. Please take the advice of the Agency and they would show you a way out.

Q 42 I stay with my son in Santa Clara. My wife stays in Fremont with my daughter. We meet very often. The Agency gives us SSA on a combined basis, as a couple. Someone told me that I can get more and so can my wife. Is it true?

Ans. Yes. Your wife and you both can get SSI on an individual basis. However this is true only if you are staying apart from your wife for good reason, and not just as a device to get more SSI. You must let the Agency know these reasons.

Q 43 I get a pension of 50 pounds from the U.K. and I earn $ 400 from my motel work. I am paid by check. Can I get SSI or Medical? I cannot afford to pay the Medicare premium. I am over 65 years of age and I am a widower.

Ans. Yes. Apply for SSI/CAPI and the Agency will scrutinize your claim as regards your immigration status and resources. If you are found eligible you will get SSI, Medi-Cal, and Medicare.

Q 44 I have a bank account in Texas in the name of Madhu Patel. I have changed my name to Madhav Merchant. I have just reached 65 years. Can I get welfare? I do not want to disclose my old account and there is no way for the Agency to find it out.

Ans. Under welfare rules you have to disclose all your income and resources. There are several penalties including imprisonment for fraud. Your social security number is the guide for the Agency to know about your old account.

Q 45   I am a widower. I have a small apartment, the rent of which is $750 plus utilities. I earn $1,800 per month, barely sufficient to maintain myself. Recently I had to incur medical expenditure. I am not 65 years of age. Can I get Medi-Cal and Medicare so as to free myself from medical expenditure?

Ans.   No, you can't get Medi-Cal benefits if you are not disabled and not 65 years of age. You will have to wait for these benefits.

Q 46   I stay with my son who does not charge me for boarding and lodging. I was getting SSI, Medi-Cal and Medicare. Recently I met with an accident and I got compensation of $20,000 after paying medical and lawyers fees. The SSI agency stopped my welfare benefits. This windfall has proved a curse to me, as I have to take medical help now and then. Can you help me to get welfare benefits?

Ans.   Consult the manager of the Agency. For the first month of receipt, you will lose your SSI. You can make use of spend down rules. As long as you are disabled, your medical benefits will not be discontinued, but you must spend down your resources as soon as possible.

Q 47 I have a small job which gives me $700 per month. I get SSI after adjustment of my income. I am 67 years of age. Recently in a side business I earned $10,000. I had many things to buy, such as a new car and a washing machine, and I spent the amount within 4 days of the receipt. But the SSI Agency stopped my SSI for one month. I want to appeal, as there is already a provision in the law for spending down. What are the chances of my success?

Ans. You have no chance of success. According to the rules, income you get during a month is taken into consideration for that month, even if you spend it. The Agency is correct in stopping SSI for one month.

Q 48 I stay in a small cottage, which my son has built by the side of his house. I pay for my food and other expenses. I cannot pay market rent to my son but can pay 2/3rd of it leaving me a small amount of my SSI for my other expenditure. How can I solve this issue and get full SSI?

Ans. Pay the full "Presumed Maximum Value" (PMV) plus $20 and consult Agency whether they are prepared to give you full SSI.

Q 49 I stay with my daughter. My pension in India is 10,000 rupees and my wife's pension is 6,000 rupees per month. We have applied for repatriation and we are likely to get about $4000 each year (as a lump sum). Will this affect our cash welfare benefits and/ or Medi-Cal benefits?

Ans. You should prepare a budget for spending the amount. You may pay back any legitimate debt. You will lose SSI benefits for the month during which you receive the annual lump sum. If you are able to bring your resources below $3000 you will continue to receive SSI and medical.

Q 50 I came here before August 22nd 1996 on a Green Card. I completed 5 years of stay in the U.S. in 1998, and I am over 65 years of age. Am I eligible for SSI?

Ans. Your sponsor signed the traditional affidavit. Since you are over 65 and are likely to be considered disabled, you would be eligible for disability benefits through the CAPI program, and for Medi-Cal, if you meet other requirements. Only if you are a citizen would you be eligible for SSI.

Ans. It's clear that the date of green card is earlier than 1996 so he must have given a traditional affidavit. After he became over 65 and disabled he is eligible for disability on CAPI, please make necessary correction.

Q 51 My wife and I get SSI, Medi-Cal and Medicare. I have been offered a job in a college on a part time basis, at $30,000 a year. Will our SSI and Medi-Cal stop if I accept the job offer and start working?

Ans. Your monthly gross income is $2,500 per month. The first $85 dollars is exempt. For every two dollars you earn, you can keep one dollar without losing SSI benefit. The remaining half is used to calculate your benefit. Even if you get only one-dollar SSI benefit, you qualify for Medi-Cal.

Q 52   My wife and I are fond of traveling. We have been here for the last 8 years but have not seen many states of the USA. My son has agreed to buy tickets for us with his credit card. Will this affect our benefits? We propose to return before 8 weeks.

Ans.   No. If your son buys tickets for domestic travel on his credit card and does not give you cash, this is not considered as your income.

Q 53   If my assets in India are fully repatriated I can get $50,000 in all. Is there any way to retain my benefits when the amount is actually received? My wife and I are both on SSI and stay with our son.

Ans.   On receipt of funds, you would lose SSI for that month at least, even if you were able to spend down your $50,000 immediately. You can spend or repay a legitimate debt, or buy an excluded resource like a car, laptop, computer, etc. Income does not result in loss of medical benefits, as there is provision for "share of cost." There are no such provisions for resources. They have to be spent down to get welfare benefits.

Q 54   My wife's job gives her $2000 net per month. I have recently become a citizen. How can I get SSI? My wife is not yet 65.

Ans.   As your wife is ineligible for SSI, an amount considered as her maintenance expenditure will be deducted from her income and the balance will be considered your unearned income. You may find out from the Agency how much SSI is admissible to you. You may be able to get Medi-Cal and Medicare, depending upon your other income and resources.

Q 55 I am getting SSI from California. I want to apply for food stamps. Should I apply to SSI office or to any other office?

Ans. You are not eligible to get food stamps in California, as you are on SSI.

Q 56 I am not yet 65 years of age. I have troubles with my eyes. I use glasses but my vision is less then 20/200. Can I get disability benefits both medical and cash?

Ans. If you get a certificate from an authorized physician to that effect, you may get both medical and cash assistance if your income and resources are within limits. Your date of getting the Green Card is also relevant. Please consult the Agency.

Q 57 I have a big house and an expensive car. Recently I lost heavily in shares and all my savings are lost. If I get SSI in 2-3 months I can survive. Will the Agency ask me to move to a smaller house and buy a cheaper car? I don't want to sell either my house or my car.

Ans. Both house and car are excluded resources for the purpose of welfare benefits. If you are otherwise eligible for SSI, the Agency will not ask you to sell the excluded resources.

Q 58   I have a joint account with my son. The money belongs to him and he had requested me not to withdraw funds without informing him. If he is not immediately available, I am supposed to inform him at the earliest. Welfare Agency refuses to give me welfare benefits. What should I do to get them?

Ans.   In order to retain your welfare benefits, you must get your name removed from the joint account. If you can prove to the satisfaction of the Welfare Agency that they are not your funds, the Agency will accept this and consider your claim if you are otherwise eligible.

Q 59   I am staying in my house and paying mortgage. I get SSI, Medi-Cal and Medicare. In order to pay mortgage I want to keep boarders. I consulted the Agency but it threatens to stop my SSI and other benefits if my income from boarders' compensation is above the prescribed limit, what should I do?

Ans.   If the income is termed as unearned, and is above the prescribed limit your SSI would stop (The rules are different for earned and unearned income). For medical benefits you may get a share of cost concession. Please consult the Agency again on this issue.

Q 60   I am 65 years of age. My son pays my medical premium to H.M.O. It is a considerable amount per month. Will it be treated as my income? Is it a monthly gift from my son? Am I eligible for welfare benefits?

Ans.   If your son directly pays the premium, it is not your income. You may be eligible to get welfare benefits if you fulfill other conditions.

Q 61   My wife and I go to India twice a year for less than a month to avoid stoppage of SSI, Medical and Medicare. My daughter-in-law who has a good amount of property in India desires that we should stay with her parents during our stay in India. She therefore pays for our tickets on her credit card. I understand that tickets bought on credit card by someone else do not count as the income of the welfare recipient. Do I understand correctly?

Ans.   This is true only for domestic travel, not for international travel. The gift of tickets for travel outside the country is considered income of the person on whose behalf the tickets are bought. You may however borrow from your daughter-in-law and pay back to her in small installments.

Q 62   My wife and I are on welfare; we do not like to stay here. We miss India very much. We go three to four times a year to India. Our son  buys tickets for us but we return within 30 days. We have not reported our departure and arrival. Have we broken the rules?

Ans.   Yes. The tickets bought by your son are a gift and are therefore your income. Even though your absence is less than thirty days, this income will reduce your SSI benefits accordingly. Please tell the Agency and appeal for a waiver of the amount. If the waiver is not granted, your SSI benefits will be reduced by the price of the tickets. To avoid this situation in the future, provide convincing proof, such as a letter to your son, that you are borrowing the amount with the intention to repay it. Then, the price of the tickets is not considered as your income.

Q 63 **My wife and I have just got our Green Cards. I have a small job, enough to maintain both of us. The company gives us medical coverage. I have $30,000 in my bank account as well as some amount in CDs. If I transfer the amount to my son today will the transfer affect our eligibility for welfare benefits? We intend to apply for them after we become citizens.**

Ans. No, It is better to transfer the amount now and by the time you get citizenship, the 36 months bar would be lifted. This is a wise decision if you make it quickly.

Q 64 **I stay with my daughter. My wife is disabled and I take care of her. Will I get any allowance as her caretaker?**

Ans. Yes, please apply to the Agency for an allowance to compensate you for the care you are giving. This is called in-home services.

Q 65 **I am 70 years of age, but I do not get cash welfare, either SSI or CAPI. I applied for general assistance and food stamps. As I am a qualified technician and have good health the Agency refuses me general assistance and food stamps. When should I appeal?**

Ans. As you are much above 65, the Agency Officer's action is not correct. You may prefer to wait and appeal after obtaining the denial letter. The letter of appeal should be sent to the Agency that denies you the benefits.

Q 66 I have completed 40 quarters (10 years) of work, but I am still 58 years old. I have developed prostate trouble and I am not able to work. Can I stop working and get my SS and other benefits?

Ans. As you are in California, you have various options. You may apply for temporary Insurance benefits, which will give you a year's relief. But you don't get medical benefits. You may apply for SS on account of disability. You may have to wait 5 months to get medical benefits, but it may be retroactive. If you are not disabled after 5 months, you don't get medical benefits. Hopefully, your employer will pay your medical bills. If your resources are below $2000 if you are single or below $3000 if you are married, you should qualify to get SSI and Medi-Cal. After 24 months of disability, you may get Medicare.

Q 67 I stay with my son and I pay him by cash my pro rata share of his expenditure. He refuses to give me a receipt and to cooperate with the Agency; as a result I have huge overpayment to repay. Can I get a waiver?

Ans. The Agency should have obtained the agreement from your son in writing. They did not. If you cannot get your son to cooperate with the Agency, it is up to the Agency to decide. You must convince them of the merits of your case. It is possible that they might give you a waiver.

Q 68 I am not yet 65 years of age. I am getting seizures almost every night. Because of my weak eyesight I can no longer work. What should I do?

Ans. Apply for disability through Social Security. It is likely that your disability may be certified. Getting SSI, CAPI or Medi-Cal benefits depends upon your immigration status, income , and resources. You should consult the Agency quickly.

Q 69 My parents are here on a visitor's visa; their visas are to expire after two months. As my wife is not keeping well I want the presence of my parents at least for a year to come. Shall I get extension of my parent's visa?

Ans. Yes. First extensions for parents are not generally refused. Please apply in time. If you are a citizen, you may also sponsor them for adjustment of status from visitors to permanent residents.

Q 70 I have a house in my wife's name here in California. I have another house in Texas, which I rent out for $500 a month. I entered this country on a Green Card before 22nd August 1996. I am completing 65 years on 5th of January 2003. How much SSI I will get? I am a citizen.

Ans. Your Texas house will be considered as a resource and you may not be able to get SSI.

Q 71 I stay with my son; I pay him my pro rata share of expenditure in cash. I get a receipt from him. The Social Security Department insists that I should pay by check. If I appeal do I stand to succeed?

Ans. There is nothing wrong in paying by cash and obtaining a receipt. Your son's responsibility is to show that amount as income in his tax return. Please advise him accordingly. You need not appeal; you can settle this matter in review, which means that your case is examined by another caseworker.

Q 72   I am suffering from deafness and my eyesight is weak. I am over 60 years of age. I want to apply for disability benefits. Is it likely that I may get them even if I am otherwise fit?

Ans.   Though there is a very strict scrutiny of disability certification, you are likely to succeed as the facts are in your favor.

Q 73   I am less than 65 years old. While I feel quite fit throughout the day I get severe backache in the afternoon after lunchtime. I take alternative medicine, as I cannot afford allopathic treatment. What are my chances of getting disability benefits both medical and cash?

Ans.   As your malady is chronic, there may be a very serious disease about which you do not know. If you apply for disability benefits, you will have to undergo a thorough medical examination, free of cost. You should apply as soon as possible.

Q 74   I was getting medical benefits in California on account of my old age. I went to India and stayed there for 10 months, I have still got my Green Card. Am I eligible to get my medical benefits resumed?

Ans.   Yes. You may however be required to give convincing reasons for your long absence of over 6 months. You have to establish your residency in California. As long as you have a Green Card, you are eligible to get medical benefits depending upon your income and resources.

Q 75   I had a high paying job. I sponsored my mother 3 years back, as my father died and there was no one to look after her. I used to pay a heavy insurance premium for her and loan her maintenance expenditure. Suddenly I developed cancer and I had to give up my job. I have resources but they are not enough to look after all the expenses of my mother. How long I shall have to wait to get welfare benefits for my mother?

Ans.   As you are disabled your resources are not deemed to be your mother's resources. Consult the Agency. They will help you to get medical and other benefits to your ailing mother.

Q 76   In addition to my own house I have a small one-room and kitchen house. I tried to sell it but both the locality and the condition of the house is such that I am not able to sell the house at a reasonable price. I am now 65 years old and now I want to apply for the SSI. Is there any way to get SSI without selling the house?

Ans.   Yes, if you can show that all reasonable efforts of selling the house have not succeeded. You may get welfare benefits with the condition that you have to continue your efforts to sell the house and report to SSI when it is sold.

Q 77 I arrived in this country in the year 1996. Since 1998 I have held a job that gives me a gross income of $1500 per month. I have completed 65 years of age. Am I eligible for medical or cash benefits?

Ans. If you have got a green card you may apply for Medi-Cal. If you are a pre 22nd August 1996 entrant, your sponsor may have given a traditional undertaking. As you have a job you may not get cash assistance or food stamps. The sponsor's liability for CAPI is raised from 5 to 10 years. As you are an old entrant you may try to apply for the benefits.

Q 78 I am getting cash assistance for immigrants under the state CAPI program. I am working in an office where I get $100 per month. I do miscellaneous work in a motel and get cash compensation nearing another $200 a month. As I was getting CAPI of $740 per month, the CAPI agency stopped my CAPI and medical benefits on the grounds that my information regarding receipt of $200 in the motel work is not true. Is there any chance of success if I appeal?

Ans. In some cases it happens that we are not able to prove beyond doubt the correctness of our statement. However if it is true, you may appeal and if you persist then you may get CAPI to the extent admissible. As regards medical benefits you may get them even if your income is more than the prescribed limit. At the most you may have to pay your share of cost.

Q 79 My son who lives in Virginia sponsored me. I am, however, staying with my daughter, who pays for my board and lodging. The department considers the property of my daughter as my property for deeming rules. If I go to Virginia I will not get any benefits as the state has no such program and does not give Medicaid to non-citizens. What should I do?

Ans. While evaluating your eligibility for welfare benefits, the Agency should consider your son's income and resources, because he is your sponsor, and should not consider your daughter's income and resources. If your son's resources are within the prescribed limits you may get welfare benefits. Due allowance will be made for your son's maintenance expenditure.

Q 80 I am getting SSI and Medi-Cal for disability, and I am also working. My employer says if I get a degree in accounting he would raise my pay, which would enable me to avoid being on welfare. To get a degree I will have to spend nearly $5000 for fees, books etc., even in a Community college. I want to save that amount from my SSI, but as I am single I am not allowed to have my bank balance exceeding $2000. Is there any way to save the amount and still retain welfare?

Ans. You can get benefit of "PASS" program. This allows you to keep more than the allowed resources to pay for job training. Please consult the Manager of SSI Agency by prior appointment for conditions of "Pass" program.

Q 81 I am a British citizen and a Green Card holder of this country. I have worked in this country for some years. I have also worked in England for some years. Can I combine the work credits in both the countries and get SSA, SSI, Medicare, and Medi-Cal etc.

Ans. You may get SSA if the combined quarters are forty or more. You may also try to get SSI. However you will not be eligible for Medicare benefits (though of course, you can always buy it yourself if you are over 65).

Q 82 **I am a Green Card holder since July 1996; during these six years I have gone to India twice, each time on a two-year permit. I had applied for my Medi-Cal benefits as well as CAPI. My Medi-Cal benefits are restored but the Agency denied my CAPI benefits. What are the chances of my getting CAPI? If I apply for CAPI will my Medi-Cal benefits be stopped? I am likely to get an adverse decision.**

Ans. It is true that the Appellate Authority has a right to review all your benefits and not necessarily just the benefits for which you have appealed. However you are a pre-1996 entrant and your sponsor is liable only for three years so there is every possibility that your CAPI benefit will be restored. Your Medi-Cal is not likely to be stopped. Medi-Cal eligibility has no relationship to sponsorship.

Q 83 **I have no property or income in this country but I have both real and personal property as well as income in India. I understand that the Consulate of India at San Francisco does not give any type of certificate as regards repatriation. As my SSI/ medical benefits are discontinued I desire to appeal. What are the rules of repatriation?**

Ans. The repatriation of income is permitted; the sale proceeds of real or personal property are not yet repatriable. The rules are changing and more and more exchange control rules are relaxed. You may on your side make genuine efforts to get repatriation to the extent admissible. You may also apply against discontinuance of your benefits. You have every chance to get your benefits resumed till you get cash in hand, which may raise your income and resources above the prescribed limit.

Q 84 I am reaching 65 years of age. I want to travel by VTA buses and I am told that seniors can have the monthly pass at concession rates and the passes are available from some senior centers or Albertson or Long Drugs stores.

VTA

What are the formalities I have to undergo for getting this pass?

Ans. You may go to VTA office at 3331 North First Street, San Jose, CA 95134-1906 and get a senior discount identity card. Please go with your passport and Green Card to prove your residency.

Q 85 My wife is not yet 65 but she has been here for the last five years. She is suffering from severe arthritis and is not able to perform her duties. Is she eligible for any benefits from the state?

Ans. Yes, if she is able to get her disability certified by the welfare department and provided her sponsor signed a traditional affidavit prior to December 1997.

Q 86 My brother who had sponsored me expired 3 years after my arrival in USA. I am over 65 years of age and have no source of income and also no resources. Can I get medical and/ or cash benefits?

Ans. Yes, you can get SSI and Medi-Cal if you came here before 22nd August 1996. If you arrived after that date you may get CAPI if you are in California. Regardless of sponsorship status, you qualify for medical benefits in California, as soon as you are over 65 years of age and you are otherwise eligible.

Q 87 I get SSI, Medi-Cal and Medicare. I have a house and a car. The cost of the car was$15,000 when I bought it. The market value is $9,000. Due to loss of vision I cannot drive the car. The caseworker has threatened to stop my SSI and other benefits if I don't dispose of this car in a month's time. She says old cars can be sold in a day. What should I do?

Ans. Please tell her that somebody drives you to the grocery store, dispensary, library, and for other necessary errands. You may not have to sell the car.

Q 88 I am on welfare. I have just become a citizen. I want to sponsor my widowed daughter. Is it possible to do so? Is it necessary for me to give up my welfare benefits before I sponsor her?

Ans. Availing welfare benefit, including cash welfare, health care, food programs and non-cash programs should not prevent you from sponsoring your relative. But you must also have a co-sponsor who has enough funds is able to support your daughter. Your co-sponsor does not have to be a citizen.

Q 89   I need to stay separately from my son and daughter-in-law. If I get a subsidized housing benefit, I can do it from my meager welfare benefits. How can I get it?

Ans.   Section 8 is a program that provides rental subsidies to low income families. The waiting list is currently closed but opens from time to time. Contact the housing authority of your county. You must be a qualified immigrant or a US citizen and fulfill the conditions of Section 8.

Q 90   When I migrated to this country I was suffering from severe backache and a weak heart. I took alternative medicine and special care of my health. When I felt much better I worked in a motel on full time basis and got compensation in cash. I must have worked about 3 years. One day while coming from motel I fell down in my bathroom and was taken to the hospital in emergency. When I got better after a month I tried to go for work but I again fell sick. As I had no other means of support I applied for disability medical allowance. The Agency refuses to grant me welfare benefits because my sickness dates from the time before I came to this country on Green Card. I had completed only 4 years of service and I am post 22nd August 1996 entrant. As I got cash allowances from the motel I am afraid to appeal against the decision. What should I do?

Ans.   You will get Medi-Cal and disability allowances because you were fit to work and actually did work after getting here. It is not your choice that you were paid in cash.

Q 91 I want to apply for citizenship but I am not well versed in English. Can I get any help from any Institute?

Ans. Please contact SIREN's office at North First Street, San Jose; they would guide you in filling the application and joining an English language class for citizenship.

Q 92 I am staying in my apartment with my wife. I had a car that I lost in an accident and as it was old I got only $1000 from the insurance company. I need a car badly as my apartment is not near any bus stand or railway station. I propose to borrow $10,000 from my friend. Will the Agency object and stop my welfare?

Ans. No. Borrowing is not considered an income. You may however have to give proof that is a genuine transaction.

Q 93 I am a Green Card holder for the last 8 years. Last year I went to India for more than 6 months. I had bought a return ticket to come back before 6 months, but my old father died and I came after 7 months. Can I get Medicare? I am on Medi-Cal and I get SSI.

Ans. Your case deserves sympathy. If you have all the proofs of what you say, you may contact the SSI agency and they may help you.

Q 94   I am on a Green Card. I am 27 years of age and I married last year to a man aged 40. Is there any way by which he can come here even on a visitor's visa?

Ans.   You may have to wait up to 3 years after your sponsorship application is approved before he can come over, because of the quota system. After three years, he can come automatically.

Q 95   My son who is very anxious that I stay in my house intends to buy a mobile home for me. I have $20,000 of my own, and he is prepared to lend me another $60,000. I can buy it outright. I expect a large sum from India when the Indian currency becomes fully convertible. My wife and I are citizens. Would the arrangement of my son have any adverse effect on my welfare? It may take 5-6 months but I need Medi-Cal badly. Can I get it with $20,000 in my bank of my own?

Ans.   If you can explain the situation to the Agency, they may consider giving you medical benefits.

Q 96   I had an old house in India. I had allowed my neighbor to use it and requested him to take care of the house. He had repaired it from time to time. He wants to move to bigger house and he sold it without my knowledge. Legal proceedings are highly expensive. As he is a travel agent he offered me an air ticket in a tour going to Australia and New Zealand. I want to settle the issue by accepting the ticket. Will this adversely affect my welfare benefits if I accept the arrangement and go on a short tour of less than 30 days?

Ans.   If this is a genuine transaction and you can prove it to the satisfaction of the Agency, it may affect your medical benefits. At the most you would lose welfare benefits for a month.

Q 97 **What is PRUCOL? Does a person on PRUCOL get any medical benefits before he gets a Green Card?**

Ans. PRUCOL refers to the status of an undocumented alien permanently residing in the United States "under color of LAW" – that is to say, as if he is a documented alien. PRUCOL requires proof that the alien is residing with the knowledge and permission of the BCIS and that the BCIS does not contemplate deportation. BCIS is unlikely to undertake the expense of deporting a harmless person. The law of PRUCOL is complex. Even if the person does not have documents necessary to prove his or her residency, he may still be given SSI and other benefits if he is otherwise eligible, without waiting for BCIS response.

Q 98 **My neighbor is an illegal (undocumented) resident. He stays with his wife, whose status is also same. Recently his wife became pregnant. Can she get medical help?**

Ans. Yes she can get restricted medical help.

Q 99 **I am a citizen, my mother died some years back and my father married a widow who had a 10 years old son. I want to sponsor my father; can I include the name of my stepmother and stepbrother in my petition?**

Ans. Yes as your stepbrother was only 10 years old at the time of your father's second marriage you can include him in your petition. You may also include your stepmother.

Q 100 My wife and I stay with my son. We have been given a room with kitchen facilities. We cook our food. I was told that as my son and his family are not eligible for food coupons and they are my household members I couldn't get food coupons. Is it true?

Ans. No. You can get food coupons if you cook your food separately and you are otherwise eligible on the basis of resources and income.

Q 101 I am 65 years of age. I am a citizen and I stay with my wife. She is also a citizen. Both of us get Medi-Cal benefits. I do not want Medicare as my neighbor who went out of country received bills for Medicare for a long time. Is it compulsory for me to apply for Medicare?

Ans. Yes, if you are getting SSI and Medi-Cal, then you must apply for Medicare if you are above 65 and eligible. It is mandatory for those who are on SSI and Medi-Cal. With Medicare, you must tell the office you are leaving the country and they stop the benefits and the payment of premium while you are gone. Your neighbor must not have done this. But he can apply for a waiver, because they cannot recover the money from your SSI

Chapter 10

Reference Cases

How to Use This Chapter

This chapter provides a number of reference cases you can use. The cases are from successful appeals against determinations of the SSA. If you are having problems, look through the cases for any that may be relevant to your situation. You can cite them in your appeal, to give weight to your own case. More information about these cases can be found in this book:

McCormick, Harvey, *Social Security Claims and Procedures*, (West Publishing, 1991)

In addition, I include a section describing some interesting appeal cases I have argued.

The chapter is divided into sections dealing with different sorts of cases:

Disability Cases

Rooney v. Shalala

Both the Social Security Act and the Due Process Clause of the Fifth Amendment require that a claimant receive an opportunity to personally appear at a hearing before a claim for disability benefit is denied. The claimant wrongfully believed he had to travel several hundred miles and gave a waiver of his right of hearing. Thereupon the Commissioner decided not to reopen previous adjudication claim. The District Court held that the commissioner's decision not to reopen the case violated the due process clause of the Fifth Amendment.

Murphy v. Gardner

Ability to do light housework is not a true TEST of ability to engage in substantial gainful activity.

Meyer v. Schweiker

A 23-minute hearing has been held to be inadequate

Bluvband v. Heckler

Where a disability claimant is handicapped by lack of counsel, ill health and an inability to speak English well, the reviewing court has a duty to make a searching investigation of the record to make certain that the claimant's right have been adequately protected.

Bradley v. Barnhart

The testimony of a non-examining Doctor was not substantial evidence, in support of denial of a claim for disability benefits.

. . . . . . The Claimant was eligible for SSI on Disability, since her stroke in 1992. In September 1997,the claimant applied for SSI under a plan for achieving self-support (Pass). Her Pass application was denied initially and upon reconsideration, the court held that the commissioner's decision denying disability claimant's proposed plan, was not based on substantial evidence, and thereby necessitated remand. Claimant's goal was to reenter the workforce as a licensed Attorney but the ALJ denied the claimant's application based on his own experience in the legal field, rejecting claimant's argument that the work of an Attorney is less physically demanding than that of a paralegal, claimant's previous position. The court found that that speculation regarding vocational pre-requisites based on the ALJ's life Experience, was evidence outside the Record and therefore inadmissible.

Szumowski v. Weinburger, Mosey v. Califono, Vega v. Califono

The ALJ must make specific findings with respect to all issues. Thus Remand was required where the primary basis of a claim for disability was pain and related problems resulting from Back conditions and the ALJ failed to make findings as to the effect of subjective pain on plaintiff's ability to work.

Failure to include findings on significant impairments in the ALJ's decision is cause for Remand, The ALJ in considering a claim for social security disability must consider the claimant's subjective evaluation of his or her own condition, and the record should show how much weight has been attributed to various items of evidence, including the claimant's subjective description

Byron v. Heckler

Treating Physician's Rule: Under the treating physician's rule, a treating physician's opinion is concerning medical disability (diagnosis and nature and degree of impairment) is binding on the finder of fact unless it is contradicted by substantial evidence

However a treating physician opinion may be rejected if it is brief, conclusory and unsupported by medical evidence. If the opinion of the treating physician is disregarded specific, legitimate reasons for this action may be set forth.

Diaz v. Secretary of Health, Education and Welfare

The presentation of additional evidence bearing "directly and substantially" on a matter in dispute generally requires reopening of a hearing. The evidence must be "new and material" and must be evaluated not by itself but in relation to evidence previously considered.

Dixon v. Heckler

The term " illiteracy" in the medical-vocational guideline, means illiteracy in English, not illiteracy in all languages. Terms like "illiterate" and "Marginal education" are not self-defining, but regulations issued by the Social Security Administration attempt to define them. Illiteracy is " the inability to read or write" Someone is considered illiterate if the person cannot read or write a simple message, such as instructions or inventory lists, even though the person can sign his or her name. Generally, an illiterate person has had little or no formal education. Marginal education means ability in reasoning, arithmetic, and language skills, which are needed to do simple unskilled types of jobs. Formal schooling at a 6th grade level or less is a marginal education.

The court declared that illiteracy turned on the inability to write, not merely on the inability to read, there was testimony that the claimant could not write, and a medical report that she could not spell. It was not enough that the claimant had six or possible seven years of formal schooling, or that the claimant could read albeit with difficulty.

Cantrell v. Secretary of Health and Human Services

Age is such an important factor that there is seldom any reason for refusing to accept a case of a claimant who is 55 or older. Virtually all of these claimants have a reasonable chance of obtaining Social Security –SSI- benefits.

Pettyjohn v. Sullivan

Residual functional capacity is the " maximum degree the person retains for 'Sustained' performance of a job." It covers " not just the ability to find a job, but the ability to hold one under actual working conditions."

Hall v. Celebrezze

The General rule with respect to degree of disability has been held that it is not necessary for the claimant to be helpless, bedridden or at " death's door" in order for him or her to establish disability.

Gardner v. Earnest and Burreel v. Finch

The so called "average man" test holds in essence that the test to determine disability is whether an average man with claimant's ailments, training, and experience could engage in substantial gainful activity. Most if not all the courts passing on the question have rejected the "average man" test.

A united State District court in rejecting the so-called abstract "average man" test stated what seems to be the accepted rule, that is, evaluation of the nature and extent of the claimant's residual ability to engage in any substantial activity must be directed to the particular person involved

Kagan v. Weinberger and Micus v. Bowen

Arthritis, in and of itself, without showing of severity test or degree of pain is not a proven disability.

The Commissioner's denial of Social Security disability benefits to a claimant suffering from systemic lupus erythematous ("lupus") was not supported by substantial evidence.

Lupus is a chronic, relapsing inflammatory disease that attacks connective tissues, and is characterized by a wide range of symptoms, including arthritis, pain in the joints, kidney and blood disorders, skin eruptions, and fever.

Frankl v. Shalala

Burden of Proof: To establish a disability claim, the claimant bears the initial burden of proof to show that he or she is unable to perform his or her past relevant work. If met, the burden of proof then shifts to the Secretary of Department of Health and Human Services (HHS) to demonstrate that the claimant retains physical residual functional capacity (RFC) to perform significant number of other jobs in the national economy that are consistent with the claimant's impairments and vocational factors such as age education, and work experience.

Applying the above rule, the Eighth U.S. Circuit Court Appeals (*47 F.3d 935, 937 (8th Cir.1995)*) held the Secretary of Department of Health and Human Services (HHS) failed to meet her burden of proving that a 52-year old farmer who sought disability insurance benefits due to his heart disease retained the capability to engage in the full range of light work. While medical evidence showed that the farmer was initially recovering well from triple bypass surgery, walking three miles day, medical evidence also demonstrated that his condition deteriorated after that time. Nothing in his medical records or in the physicians' later progress notes was inconsistent with his complaints of fatigue at the time of the hearing.

Smith v. Shalala

A claimant was entitled to an award of social security disability benefits even though a vocational expert had testified that the claimant could work as a hand-packer or production assembler. The Dictionary of Occupational Titles establishes that those jobs were beyond the capability of somebody with the claimant's undisputed physical limitations. When expert testimony conflicts with the DOT, the DOT controls

Washington v. Apfel

A claimant with a high school education and history of unskilled employment, whose application for social security disability insurance benefits was denied by an Administrative Law Judge 22 days prior to the claimant's 55th birthday was entitled to the benefits retroactive to that birthday; the ALJ improperly failed to recognize that the claimant would shortly be of advanced age.

Goldberg v. Kelly

The termination of AFDC and SSI benefits requires a pre-termination hearing. The Goldberg rule (no termination of benefits without prior hearing) applies both with respect to a hearing officer and/or proceedings before the Appeals council. As soon as the intimation is received about rejection of a disability claim or any other claim, it is expedient to apply for appeal immediately within 10 days at the latest to get the benefit of the principles of Goldberg case even if it does not directly apply.

Baker v. Apfel (1998)

Because the plaintiff could not return to his former work, the burden shifted to the Commissioner to show that he is capable of performing jobs that exist in significant number in the national economy. The Commissioner failed to carry this burden because the hypothetical question posed to the vocational expert did not reflect the plaintiff's impairments and capabilities. The plaintiff's migraine headaches required him to go to the emergency room for injection. This could cause him to miss work several days a month. The vocational expert should consider this excessive absenteeism. The decision denying benefits was reversed and the case remanded for further proceedings.

Smith ex rel. Enge v. Massanari (2001)

A determination by Commissioner of Social Security Administration that child's asthma did not amount to severe impairment, and that child was not entitled to Supplemental Security Income (SSI) benefits on basis of disability, was not supported by substantial evidence, where Commissioner failed to set forth reasons for implicitly rejecting opinion of child's treating physician who diagnosed her with chronic severe bronchial asthma, and Commissioner failed to properly consider testimony of child's mother who said that, due to child's asthma, child was frequently hospitalized, child missed school about seven days per month and had to repeat first grade, and that child was unable to run or walk long distances.

The court remanded the case to allow the Commissioner to go beyond step two in three-step process to determine if child was entitled to Supplemental Security Income (SSI) benefits.

Muncy v. Apfel

It has been held by one court that the plaintiff's failure "to sit and squirm" with pain during a 36 minutes hearing cannot be dispositive of his credibility. The ALJ improperly discredited the plaintiff's complaints of pain, the decision terminating benefits was reversed and the case was remanded for further evaluation.

SSI Reference Cases

Sober-Perez v. Schweiker

It has been held that the equity protection clause did not require the Social Security Administration to give Bilingual notices as the procedures giving notices in English only alleged to be discriminatory were based on language and not upon ethnic origin.

A valid, historical basis and modern rationale for conducting Government affairs in English was clear, since the national language of the United States is English.

Toner v. Schweiker and Polette v. Chater

Sham financial arrangements are devices used to avoid excessive earnings restrictions. While it was held that an individual may arrange his financial affairs in such a manner as to render him eligible for retirement insurance benefits, if the business transactions are bona fide. In a Missouri case it was held that the claimant was had not retired, because he continued to work after his salary was stopped and without any additional work or responsibility shouldered by his wife the wife's salary was doubled. The claimant was not found to be credible.

Cornelius v. Sullivan

In a case of baby sitting the court had upheld the constitutionality of relevant regulations excluding parent –child domestic employment from coverage except under certain circumstances. A mother who was denied credit for the money she earned as a baby-sitter for her married daughter's child in her own home during a two-year period argued unsuccessfully that the provision and regulations violated equal protection in that they arbitrarily and irrationally distinguished her for the purpose of denying retirement benefits on the basis of her daughter's marital status. The excepted situations that congress had decided to cover reasonably were based not on marital status but on the fact that a parent who was a sole provider and caregiver because of divorce, death or disablement was likely to have a legitimate need for domestic services provided by a parent or another.

Tyson v. Heckler

Statutory exclusion from employment of services by a child less than 21 years of age employed by a child's father or mother has been held as constitutional. The court found that the age of majority in many states is now 18 rather than 21,does not affect constitutionality. Reduction in the age of Majority did not necessarily reduce or even affect the likelihood of fraud between parents and children when children seek employment, and reduction of the age limitation is a choice for congress. In addition, the court noted that the fact that Congress does not exclude from coverage employment of a parent by a child not the coverage of children employed by their parents' wholly owned corporation or partnership, does not render the statute unconstitutional. Congress reasonably could have concluded that less likelihood collision exists with employment by partnerships and corporations, as many such organizations are not wholly owned, and consequently people other than a child's parent play a role in hiring the child. Such a difference in treatment is not arbitrary and does not render the statute unconstitutional.

Krishnan ex rel. Deviprasad v. Massanari

Disqualification based on six months absence from the U.S: In Krishnan ex rel. Deviprasad v. Massanari, the district Court held that the limitation on aliens residing outside the United States for more than six months being ineligible for Social Security disability benefits does not violate due process. The court stated that the limitation bears a rational relationship to legitimate Government interests of regulating the relationship between the united states and alien visitors, and that programs should primarily benefit citizens and certain non-citizens who have (lived in United States for substantial period of time; (2) who have paid into program for substantial period of time;(3) who are citizens of country that has reciprocal rule; and/or (4) are governed under a treaty regarding payment of social insurance benefits.

Treaty Status With India

The U.S. treaty status in *Krishnan* was of some importance to the holding in that case. The court explained that a "treaty country" is one where application of the general rule would violate a United States treaty obligation. The court stated that India is not a treaty country. India was also not considered a " reciprocal' country because it has been found to have no social insurance system of general application that pays periodic benefits to the U.S.

Banuelos v. Apfel

Substantial evidence supported determination that the recipient of Social Security Disability benefits had sufficient assets to repay. Though he was not at fault and his assets did not generate income used by recipient for living expenses, the assets had liquidation value that could be utilized in order to provide repayment.

Setian v. Apfel

A Massachusetts case involved the issue whether recovery of a $41,000 overpayment would defeat the purpose of the act. "Defeat the purpose of the act" means that repayment would deprive the person of Income needed for ordinary living expenses. ---An overpaid individual was not required to use all his non-income assets to repay an overpayment. A claimant was entitled to retain sufficient monetary resources in order to be prepared for emergencies.

Rulings: SSR 75-14a: Proof of age – Evaluation of Evidence

http://www.ssa.gov/OP_Home/rulings/oasi/03/SSR75-14-oasi-03.html

Go to: http://www.ssa.gov/OP_Home/rulings/rulings.html for a list of SSA rulings. An index is available to help you find rulings of interest.

The claimant was born in Georgia and no civil or religious records of his birth exist. He stated that his Aunt and mother both told him he was born on January 26; 1910.He has used this date of birth consistently since 1944. While the 1920 census record and record from the elementary school showed his date of birth as January 26 1913, all the records from 1948 to 1973 indicated his date of birth as 26 January 1910. It was held that the higher probative value should be given to the earliest written records.

Expert medical evidence may be used to establish Age. Thus it has been held that an Administrative law judge failed to give proper consideration to medical evidence that a claimant of Chinese ancestry was 12 years older than her documentation reflected, and was thus eligible for retirement benefits. Reports of independent examining gerontologist, as well as the claimant's treating physician and dentist, verified the claimant's testimony that she misstated her age to survive in the job market in post-war Hong Kong and continued to misrepresent her age at the time of her immigration for fear that any attempt to correct the erroneous date would result in denial of immigration or subsequent deportation. The Administrative Law Judge also should not have rejected a Chinese birth certificate and affidavits of the claimant's family members.

If the age established previously makes the applicant ineligible for SSI, the applicant is given opportunity to submit new evidence to support an allegation that he or she is at least 65.

The evidence of age requirements for individual filing for SSI who are age 65 to 68 are same as for social security. Payments may be initiated however based on evidence of probative value that reasonably supports the allegation while required evidence is being obtained as above.

In this age range, less probative evidence may be sufficient as age proof. Thus documentary evidence at least three years old, which supports the alleged age of an individual age 68 or older, is what is required.

Rulings SSR 82-26: Non-Exempt Property

Claimant and his wife lived together in a rented house and owned a piece of land on which there was a two room structure and a trailer which they used to vacation approximately one month each year.

Held: The property is not excluded because it is not his principal place of residence and it is therefore countable and he is not eligible.

Rulings SSR 82-28a: Grandchildren and Income Deeming

The claimant who lives in the same household with her husband and their three grand children, applied for SSI as a disabled individual. Neither the husband nor the grandchildren are eligible for SSI. Claimant was denied benefits because the income deemed available to her from her husband exceeded the statutory limit.

Held: "Ineligible child" applied only to natural or adopted children and not to grandchildren. The maintenance expenditure of the grandchildren could not be deducted from the husband's income.

Medi-Cal Reference Cases

Armstrong v. Palmer

Denial of Medicaid Benefits based on SSA finding of Non-Disability.

Medicaid Benefits may be denied based upon a finding on non-disability by SSA. In accordance with SSI rules a state Medicaid Agency may deny Medicaid Benefits to a claimant who has been found by the Social Security administration to be not disabled for purposes of SSI Income Eligibility.

Norris v. Schweiker

An ALJ erred in incorporating into his findings the opinions of a non-examining physician, which appeared to have been unsupported guesses.

Appeals I Have Argued

Case 1: Disability

Shantaben, a culinary expert staying at Los Angeles, was suffering from back pain, time and again. The pain was more severe in the afternoon probably due to the time spent in the kitchen. Especially as she had no medical coverage, she used to take alternative medicine for immediate help.

I advised her to apply for disability medical benefits and disability SSI benefits. At the time of the interview with the caseworker she was asked to state what work she could do and what other work she could not do. Cooking was a very sensitive subject for her and she was proud of her expertise in cooking, both qualitative and quantitative. She replied "I can cook for 500 people at a time." I was present as her interpreter. The sympathetic caseworker was confused. How she would process the claim of disability on face of the factual information given to her. I explained the difference between what one can do and what one should do. I requested her to get Shantaben examined by a strict and expert physician. After various tiring clinical tests it was found out that Shantaben was about to contract cancer. She was advised bed rest and medical and financial benefits were admitted to her without demur.

Most of the people of Asian Indian origin make this mistake. They themselves decide whether they are medically fit or not. Our culture and heritage teach us to put complete faith in God. That is the right thing to do but it has some adverse effect. We have also to take it into consideration.

Case 2: Cash Payment for Work Done

My friend Kaushik was a life-long patient. Before he migrated to this country he had innumerable medical complaints. He was a post 8/22/96 entrant. When he applied for disability medical and cash benefits, he was asked about the time when the disability occurred. He said it was an old complaint and he did not know the exact time and date it first occurred. His disability was rejected. As he had no other means to support himself he took a small job in a motel and was paid by cash and not by check. He worked for about 6 months and one day while returning from duty he felt dizzy and had a fall in his bathroom. He was at once taken to hospital and after a week he was released. He did not go to work thereafter. I advised him to apply again for disability. The claim was rejected. He appealed and I was authorized to represent him. The Agency argued that the disease was old and he was not eligible for benefits. Moreover his sponsor had given a traditional affidavit and the rules said "For 5 years the sponsor is liable irrespective of the form in which the affidavit was given." I argued that he had become fit to work; he had actually worked in a motel. The fact that he received cash instead of check is not a relevant issue. I also argued that if the applicant becomes disabled, the sponsor is not liable after 3 years. The Honorable Judge accepted my contention and granted the claim.

The point at issue is that it is irregular but not illegal to accept cash for work done. The Administrative Law Judge may at his discretion ignore the irregularity taking into account the factual situation. Had Kaushik maintained that he did voluntary work at the motel his claim would not have been admitted. My advice to the welfare claimant/recipient is: if you go before the welfare department, tell the truth. The truth may not harm you as much as you imagine.

Case 3: Property That Cannot be Sold

My friend Mohan had a house in India and no other property. The estimated value of the house was $8,000. He was in receipt of CAPI as well as Medi-Cal. At the time of review the caseworker advised him to sell the house, bring the proceeds to this country and spend them down bringing them below $3,000 (he had an ineligible spouse living with him). Only then would his benefits be resumed. I advised him to appeal against the denial. The government of India has since relaxed the rules in favor of repatriation. However the rules as they were at the time of appeal, indicated that the claim was incorrectly denied.

The rules are clear on the point that resources are considered excluded and not available to the welfare claimant/recipient if he cannot convert them into cash and make use of them. The house Mohan had in India had first to be sold and the cash proceeds were to be brought here with the permission of the Reserve Bank. Even after the proceeds are received, there is provision to spend then down and keep the proof that they were spent down. If the amount of the sale proceeds is spent down and the cash amount is brought below $3,000 for a couple and $2,000 for individual, the claim can be sustained.

Below is the relevant extract from the judgment of the Administrative Law Judge:

> "The regulations governing the CAPI program clearly indicate that the definition of resources for CAPI purposes is the same as the one used for SSI/SSP. The cited code of Federal Regulations (CFR) section 20 CFR 416. 1201 (a) (1) indicates that, for purposes of determining whether a resource may be considered. The federal government determines if the property rights can be liquidated. If the property rights cannot be liquidated, the property will not be considered a resource of the individual. In this case, the claimant may well be able to sell his apartment in India. The testimony indicates that he may not be able to transfer the liquidated proceeds of the sale of the property. The Administrative Law Judge discussed this case with the CAPI analyst in Sacramento who concurs that, under existing Law, the value of the apartment in India is not available and may not be considered in determining the claimant's ongoing eligibility for CAPI. The county's action to discontinue CAPI, effective March 31, 2001 was therefore incorrect and cannot be sustained. The Administrative Law Judge notes the concern of the claimant's representative that not all Indian Nationals are treated

consistently. As she does not have other cases within her jurisdiction, she is unable to review county action in those cases.

Order

The claim is granted.

Santa Clara County shall rescind its action to terminate claimant's CAPI program benefits and shall restore claimant to his CAPI benefits, effective March 31, 2001, as otherwise eligible. The county shall provide the claimant with all appropriate retroactive benefits effective March3, 2001 as otherwise eligible."

Case 4: Disability in Those Over 55 Years Old

Mrs. Desai was disabled as per the certificate given by the attending physician. The norms laid down for determining disability indicated that the disability was not beyond doubt and the claim was initially rejected. The claimant was advised to appeal. The Honorable Administrative Law Judge accepted my contention that the physician's certificate is a *prima facie* proof of disability. The Agency was free to ask for a second opinion but it was not proper to reject the claim only on the basis of the norms. If the claimant is above 55 years of age, the policy is not to insist that he or she is fit to do gainful work. Most of the caseworkers ignore these guidelines. The claimant/recipient should therefore bear in mind this important issue before accepting the rejection.

Case 5: Unexpected Recovery from Disability

Gaurav was a student in a private college, which does not provide for medical coverage. After a couple of months of his admission in the college, he became seriously ill. His disease needed surgery and the treatment was protracted for nearly a year. The doctors found him fit only before the end of the year. He was however advised to skip one more term so that his concentration in studies would not affect his health. He applied for disability and the claim was initially rejected. On appeal I contended that though he was certified medically fit a little before the completion of a year, the advice of the doctor to skip a term indicated that he was not completely fit to resume the work that he was doing before. The question of his capability to do any lighter gainful work was not considered appropriate for a student. The rule *inter-alia* provides that if at the time of initial malady the disease is likely to be prolonged for a year, the fact that expert medical technology and treatment and care he received at the hospital made him fit much before the end of the year, though a tribute to the medical profession, may not be made use of to reject the claim of disability. The claim was granted, the enormous medical bill was covered under Medi-Cal, for which he was considered eligible, and a lot of anxiety was over.

The issue to be borne in mind is not to be unnerved by the initial rejection. If it is genuinely felt that the claimant is disabled, the appeal process is always open to correct the error of judgment of the Agency Guidelines and Regulations.

Chapter 11
States Other Than California

According to 2000 Census report, the population of North America is a little more than 280 Millions (28 Crores). California accounts for 34 Millions (3 Crores and 40 lakhs). The Asian Indians in California are as many as 315 thousands (3 lakhs and 15 thousand). On the basis of the national average of 12 percent, the elderly population of Asian Indians in California is about 40,000.

Due to decentralization and delegation of responsibilities to states and counties, it is not possible to give accurate information about the welfare program in states other than California. The Federal eligibility and responsibility rules are the same in all states. Detailed information about them is available at the web-site www.ssa.gov.

Some states provide optional monthly supplement to help people meet needs not fully covered by federal SSI payments. Some states provide optional monthly supplements to all persons eligible for SSI benefits. Others may limit them to certain SSI recipients such as the blind or residents of care facilities, or they may extend payments to people ineligible for SSI because of excess income.

No Supplementary Payments

The following six states have no provision for optional supplementary payments

* Arkansas
* Georgia
* Kansas
* Mississippi
* Tennessee
* West Virginia

Medicaid Eligibility in Different States

States can supplement the Federal medical assistance to the needy or not, and they can use Federal guidelines for eligibility or not. This section provides a brief summary of the policies of the different states.

It was possible to furnish this information as updated up to July 2002 due to special indulgence shown by Sheila Barber of Baltimore from the office of the Associate Commissioner for Research Evaluation and Statistics

Use State Guidelines, not Federal

The following states follow their own guidelines in giving medical aid to SSI recipients:

* Hawaii
* Illinois
* Minnesota

- New Hampshire
- Missouri
- North Dakota
- Ohio
- Oklahoma
- Virginia

All other state follows Federal guidelines. The state of Connecticut however follows both federal and state guidelines.

Medically Needy Program

The following states have a *Medically Needy* program:

- Arizona
- Arkansas
- Colorado
- Delaware
- Maryland
- Massachusetts
- Iowa
- Kentucky
- Louisiana
- Maine
- District of Columbia
- New Jersey
- Pennsylvania
- Rhode Islands
- South Dakota
- Tennessee
- Washington
- West Virginia
- Wyoming

The remaining states have no such program.

Concurrent Eligibility States

Concurrent eligibility is eligibility for both Medicaid and SSI. In some states Medicaid eligibility is automatic when an individual is approved for SSI. In other states Medicaid eligibility involves a separate and independent determination of eligibility, which may be made under contract with a state by SSI or by the state itself.

The following States impose at least one eligibility criteria more restrictive than the SSI program. They are called "209(b)" states:

* Connecticut
* Hawaii
* Illinois
* Indiana
* Minnesota
* Missouri
* New Hampshire
* North Dakota
* Ohio
* Oklahoma
* Virginia

SSI Criteria States

The following states use SSI eligibility criteria for Medicaid but they make their own Medicaid determinations or ask SSI to do it. They are called "SSI criteria States":

* Alaska
* Idaho
* Kansas
* Nebraska
* Nevada
* Northern Mariana Islands
* Oregon
* Oregon
* Utah

The Rest of the States

The rest of the states agree to let SSI make Medicaid determinations. To do so, each state enters a "1634 agreement" with SSA, named after the appropriate provision of the Social security Act. In these "1634 states," SSA determines whether an individual is eligible for Medicaid beginning with the day he or she becomes eligible for SSI payments or federally admissible state supplemental payments (SSP). Medicaid eligibility continues for the same period for which the individual remains eligible for these payments or for 1619(b) payments. This can be the first day of the month or, if prorating applies, the same day the individual meets all eligibility criteria for SSI/ SSP payments and Medicaid.

Endorsements

The following businesses have been helpful to me in my work with seniors.

RAO
IMMIGRATION SERVICES
Making your American Dream Come True!

- Visitor Visa
- Political Asylum
- Student Visa
- Green Card
- Business Visa
- Relative Visa
- Investor Visa
- Citizenship
- Crew Visa
- Labor Certification
- U.S. Immigrations
- Support Affidavit
- Company Transfers
- Status Adjustment
- Indian Passport
- Adoption

Indian Passport & Miscellaneous Consular Services

REASONABLE FEES & GUARANTEED SATISFACTION

Member: American Immigration Lawyers Association

We speak Gujarati/Hindi/Punjabi/Urdu

U.S.A.	INDIA
18520 ½ S. Pioneer Blvd.	6, Kolsawala Building
Suite #202, Artesia CA 90701	Dinbai tower, Lal Darwaja
TEL: 562-403-1646	Ahmedabad 380001
Fax: 562-403-1647	**TEL: 91-79-550-2261**
E-mail: raoinssvcs@yahoo.com	**Fax: 91-79-550-5251**
rai4ubs@alk.com	E-mail: rajputlaw@hotmail.com

FOR **FREE** CONSULTATION **CALL NOW**

INDEX